Charles W. Burpee

The Military History of Waterbury

From the Founding of the Settlement in 1678 to 1891

Charles W. Burpee

The Military History of Waterbury
From the Founding of the Settlement in 1678 to 1891

ISBN/EAN: 9783337139469

Printed in Europe, USA, Canada, Australia, Japan

Cover: Foto ©ninafisch / pixelio.de

More available books at **www.hansebooks.com**

THE MILITARY HISTORY

OF

WATERBURY,

FROM THE FOUNDING OF THE SETTLEMENT IN 1678 TO 1891, TOGETHER WITH A LIST OF THE COMMISSIONED OFFICERS AND THE RECORDS OF THE WARS; CONTAINING ALSO AN OUTLINE OF ALL THE CHANGES IN THE MILITARY ORGANIZATION OF THE STATE.

BY

CHARLES W. BURPEE.

If we desire to secure peace, one of the most powerful instruments of our rising prosperity, it must be known that we are at all times ready for war.

GEORGE WASHINGTON.

INAUGURAL ADDRESS, DECEMBER 3, 1793.

NEW HAVEN, CONN.:
THE PRICE, LEE & ADKINS CO., PRINTERS,
206-210 MEADOW STREET.
1891.

Entered according to Act of Congress, in the year 1891,

BY CHARLES W. BURPEE,

In the Office of the Librarian of Congress, at Washington.

Introductory.

A live military spirit is an indication of the healthy condition of the general community. In time of war it is the safeguard; in time of peace, when that spirit is purely voluntary and spontaneous, it stands for the red blood, the loyal heart, the active but obedient mind and the ready hand of the young men. Improvements in the enginery of war tend to reduce war to a minimum, but it is the well-established alertness of the people themselves which produces the primary and thus the greatest effect.

What the citizen soldier can do in time of need it remained for America to demonstrate most satisfactorily, in the war of the Revolution and in the war of the Rebellion. And of all the States, the world does honor to Connecticut for standing foremost in this work of demonstration. It is with honest pride, then, that we consider the position which Waterbury has held in this State. From the time when the handful of Farmington pilgrims, armed against the savages, made their camp fire in the meadows of the Naugatuck, the men of the community have ever held themselves in readiness for the call of duty. As the forefathers knew that, by keeping the gun within reach while they plowed, their hearthstones were safest, thus the people of to-day realize that the protection which makes possible their industries and which builds their houses depends first of all upon the militia, which is themselves. Not only were Waterbury men found in the ranks in the wars against the Indians or against usurping white men; they were found also in the councils which devised the plans for preventing such wars by making soldier and citizen synonymous.

In writing the military history of Waterbury there has been no call to borrow sounding phrases; the mere records, the lists of names and deeds, are far more potent than language of eulogist. The only fear is that in the chaotic period of the earlier days, when records were very faulty, an occasional name may have been omitted in the appended list of officers.

WATERBURY, CONN., Feb. 1, 1891.

Table of Contents.

		PAGE
I.	COLONIAL DAYS	5
II.	THE REVOLUTIONARY WAR	13
III.	DAYS OF THE TWENTY-SIXTH REGIMENT	20
IV.	THE WAR OF 1812	22
V.	FIRST FLANK AND BATTALION COMPANIES	26
VI.	FOLLOWING THE FLOOD WOODS	31
VII.	THE MEXICAN WAR	35
VIII.	REORGANIZATION OF THE MILITIA—COMPANY H	37
IX.	THE REBELLION	49
X.	IN THE CONNECTICUT NATIONAL GUARD	66
	RECORD IN INDIAN AND FRENCH WARS	78
	RECORD IN THE REVOLUTION	78
	RECORD IN THE WAR OF 1812 AND MEXICAN WAR	80
	RECORD IN THE REBELLION	81
	COMMISSIONED OFFICERS OF THE MILITIA SINCE 1678	84
	ROLLS OF COMPANIES A AND G	97–98

I. Colonial Days.

The martial spirit possessed our ancestors and they recognized the glory of a military life. As Henry Bronson has said: "There was a demand for warriors, and warriors of a superior order came forth. * * * Military titles were in high repute among the colonists. They were preferred to civil or ecclesiastical honors. A corporal was on the road to distinction. * * * A captain was necessarily a man of great influence whose opinion was taken in all the weighty concerns of the town. Few aspired to the exalted rank of major." By a law of the colony, all men between 16 and 60 were subject to bear arms, with a few exceptions in favor of those engaged in vocations necessary to the whole community. A certain number of days each year was devoted to the inspection of the arms and ammunition in every house, and to military drill of a rude sort, while a guard of no less than eight men did duty in every town on Sundays.

The settlers of Mattatuck, on their second visit from Farmington, quickly perceived that they must have some kind of martial organization to protect themselves from the Indians who were crowded back from Derby or making sallies from remote northern territory.

In 1678, the year of the regular settlement, two armed men were appointed to keep lookout from the hills. In 1680, the men had established a system of signals which should call them together as one body, and they were accustomed to meet to devise the best means to repel an attack. The house of Thomas Judd, Sr., "of Waterbury," an armory in itself, was the meeting place, and on his kitchen floor probably many a defensive campaign was marked out. It was there that the militia in which the city rejoices to-day had its inception. Two years later, when the population was not yet 200 and there was no great danger, the pioneer soldiery numbered 24. Recognizing the need of some head to their ambitious organization, they went before the General Court which appointed two sergeants, the highest office the law would allow for this number of men. Then, as continually down to the close of the Revolution, the General Court or Assembly filled all military offices. Thomas Judd, Sr., and John Stanley were the choice for sergeants.

Slowly the numbers increased until in 1689 there were 35 men, which warranted the appointment of a lieutenant. John Stanley was the man selected. His chief duty was to see that all citizens were well armed, and that there were at least 32 whom he could call together at any time for special duty. All must bring their arms to "meeting" when ordered.

The pay allowed by the colony for active service was 25 shillings per week for captains, 18 for lieutenants, 15 for ensigns and 9 for privates. A sergeant-major in each county had the direct supervision of the train bands. There was no higher office than this one which was established in 1672.

Indian alarms becoming more frequent, the General Court in 1690 established a military watch throughout the colony, on which all persons whatsoever (Indians and negroes excepted) upwards of sixteen years were compelled to serve. In April "fortifications" were ordered in each town. Waterbury hospitality was put to its utmost test by bands of soldiers passing through on scouting expeditions, and as many of the husbandmen accompanied them on these expeditions, the crops were left uncared for. It was a hard battle for existence without and within. In recognition of the town's fidelity and sacrifices, the General Court, in 1691, kindly allowed it "the present county rate toward erecting a house for public worship." Thus the local church may be said to have found its beginning in martial valor.

The exact condition of affairs in one locality cannot be understood without keeping in mind the course of events in the colony as a whole. We can well imagine with what indignation the sturdy "centinels" heard that Sir William Phips, in 1692, lately landed in Boston, had sent word that thereafter he would be commander-in-chief of Connecticut's forces, and with what applause they received the news that the offer had been rejected by the authorities at Hartford, who were determined to stand by their charter rights. And again they must have smiled grimly when the following year they heard the story of how Gov. Benjamin Fletcher of New York had come to Hartford to take command only to meet with a more emphatic rebuff. The militia, though still without organization, was beginning to be an important factor in matters of state. There was also now another goal for individual ambition, for in 1689 there had been created the office of lieutenant-colonel, for some localities, equal in rank to that of sergeant-major. He and the other officers were subject to the call of a committee of safety appointed for each county. Waterbury was in Hartford county. So strict was discipline becoming that bands must train six times a year, between March and November, and a severe penalty was imposed upon any soldier who should spoil or sell arms or ammunition, and upon citizens who should buy of them. Those harboring veterans should be allowed four pence per meal and 4s. 6d. per week for board; they must take no more. Fines for absence on training days went toward the purchase of drums and colors; if insufficient, the balance was collected from the town. In 1697 where companies were near enough together to form a general organization called a regiment, sergeant-majors were made majors, with power to call together commissioned officers once a year to discuss the management of the militia. In 1702 it was decreed that several companies in each town should be counted as one post on general muster. Majors were forbidden to hold a captain's commission. When it was necessary to impress men into the service, the majors could hand a list of names to the constable and he must bring in the men. After 1704 commissioned officers were not allowed "to give up office without consent of the governor or General Assembly, under penalty of being put in the ranks and made corporals."

The colony already had come to feel that the Indian was the least of its enemies and that its militia must be developed into an arm capable of warding off any blow. Gov. Treat was himself a soldier; indeed, he owed his office to his skill and valor in the King Philip campaign. In 1690, Gov. Bradstreet of Massachusetts had sent to him for assistance. At the request of Gov. Leisler of New York, Capt. Fitz John Winthrop had led his Connecticut forces for the invasion of Canada, destined to return since others had not dared to follow where his men led. The royal governor of New York, Benjamin Fletcher, after failing to take forcible possession of the militia of this colony had resorted to strategem, asking the General Assembly to acknowledge the king's right to appoint a commander-in-chief. The Assembly promptly refused, Gov. Treat declined the commission offered him and Gov. Fletcher gave up in despair. The Yankee militia were ever an independent body. They willingly sent men to King William's war against the French in 1689 and to Queen Anne's in 1702, as they did to King George's in 1744 and to the old French and Indian wars of 1755-63, but they always retained control over themselves.

When the bands turned out six times each year for drill, work was forsaken, and men, women and children came forth to celebrate. One writer says: "The enjoyment which they experienced in watching the maneuvers of the soldiers and the games of cudgel, back-sword, fencing, running, leaping, wrestling, stool ball, nine-pins and quoits was enhanced by sharing the spectacle with the multitude, meeting old friends and making acquaintances."

It was the Indians, urged on by the French, who most disturbed the Waterbury people. On April 9, 1700, when Thomas Judd was lieutenant (appointed in 1695), they voted to fortify Ensign Timothy Stanley's house, and four years later another, that of the Rev. John Southmayd. April 15, 1703, a town stock of ammunition was provided by the Assembly, with Stanley, then a lieutenant, as keeper. In May of the following year, the Assembly designated eight towns as frontier towns, including Waterbury, with ten men in garrison in Waterbury, Danbury, Woodbury and Simsbury, while New Haven and Fairfield county men acted as scouts. These towns were ordered to have fortified houses in 1707, and " to keep a good scout out every day, of two faithful and trusty men." A year later it was ordered, in an act "for the encouragement of military skill and good discipline," that the committee of safety in Hartford should establish garrisons in certain towns, one of which was Waterbury, at the charge of the colony or of the respective towns, as the committee should order. Two garrison forts were so established in Waterbury at the expense of the colony, and one at the expense of the town, one at the Rev. Mr. Southmayd's house, one at Lieut. Stanley's, and the third at John Hopkins's. To encourage men to take the aggressive, big prices were paid for Indian scalps and prisoners down to the year 1746. Each town was also obliged to keep on hand a certain number of snow shoes and moccasins.

The alarm increasing, the Assembly, being petitioned, appointed a committee of war in 1710, with power to send reinforcements from New Haven county in case of need. But peace was declared in 1713.

Perhaps it was due to all these precautions that Waterbury was unmolested save for the killing of a man named Holt, and for the capture of Jonathan Scott and his two sons.

Now the required membership of 64 had been reached, and in 1715 a captain was allowed. Deacon Thomas Judd, son of the late lieutenant, was crowned with the honor, than which there could be few greater in the minds of his compatriots. John Hopkins, ensign, soon became lieutenant.

One more step toward general consolidation of the colony's forces had been taken in 1708 when the governor was made regularly the commander-in-chief. That year, also, it was decreed that thereafter men over 55 need not be required to do active service. The year after the close of the war, in 1714, the mounting of a guard on Sunday was done away with. In 1722, the regimental offices of colonel and lieutenant-colonel were established, though there were still no regiments as such. That year, when Dr. Ephraim Warner was captain here and all were held in readiness to go to the aid of the frontier town of Litchfield if need be, Gov. Burnett of New York, like Phips and Fletcher before him, demanded the command of the Connecticut militia and, like them, he met with a prompt refusal. The population of the State in 1730 was 38,000 and the militia, counting men between 16 and 65, numbered 8,500.

William Judd had then become captain of Waterbury's contingent, which was assuming such large proportions that by 1732 the Assembly ordered two companies, the second to be commanded by Timothy Hopkins. Nothing more plainly marked the prosperity of the town, which, it may be noted in passing, had been annexed to New Haven County in 1728. After 1736, men over 50 were exempt from active service, though still counted in the militia.

The management of so many different train bands even when brought together by counties had become so difficult that at the October session in 1739 the General Assembly decided to establish regiments and the number was fixed at 13. The militia numbered 3,480, divided into 47 companies. The Waterbury, Wallingford, Durham and Southington companies constituted the Tenth regiment. The colonel was to exercise the power previously granted to the major of each county and the governor should be captain-general. The officers of the Tenth were James Wadsworth colonel, Benjamin Hall lieutenant-colonel and Thomas Miles major. Col. Humphrey Bland's tactics were ordered as official in 1743, but the general principle more closely followed was that primitive one of "every man for himself."

But whatever the tactics, the fighting qualities of the men were unquestioned. The Louisburg campaign, in 1745, found the Waterbury men ready, and the Assembly selected Samuel Hickcox to be captain of a company sent to Cape Breton as re-inforcements.

When England declared war against France ten years later, and the colonies were again involved, there were three companies in Waterbury. John Brunson was appointed captain of the third in 1751, and Jacob Blakeley lieutenant. Two regiments being organized to do regular duty in protecting the territory of the colonies from French invasion, Gershom Fulford was made second lieutenant of the fourth company of the Second regiment, Elizur Goodrich colonel. The Rev. Mark Leavenworth went with the regiment as chaplain. In 1759, the year previous to his appointment, the number of regiments in the field had been increased to four and Timothy Clark was a second lieutenant in the Third regiment. There was a goodly number of Waterbury privates behind these officers.

To further facilitate the handling of the militia the office of brigadier-major was established in 1759. Benjamin Hall had succeeded to the colonelcy of the Tenth militia, in 1755.

At the outbreak of the war with France, Lord Halifax had proposed in Parliament that the governors of the colonies and two delegates from each colony have authority to direct the military and draw money for the expense from England, which should afterwards be repaid by taxes on the colonists. All the colonies refusing, the project was dropped. Phineas Lyman was major-general commanding the Connecticut troops in the Lake Champlain campaign. It was there that the contempt of the colonists for the British regulars reached its climax and the Waterbury men agreed in the general condemnation of them. Thus it was that, seeing that the most of the burden must fall upon the colonists, the Assembly was aroused by William Pitt's earnest letter in 1758 and voted 5,000 more men, to follow the cowardly Abercrombie. Among them was Capt. Eldad Lewis, at the head of a company of 34 Waterbury men.; Samuel Judd was his first lieutenant.

After the close of this war, in 1763, new companies were organized in the Northbury (Plymouth) and Westbury (Watertown) districts of the town and Aaron Harrison was appointed captain of the company in the Northbury parish.

In 1767 the number of regiments was increased to 14, to be further increased to 15 in 1769, to 16 in 1771, to 22 in 1774, to 24 in 1775 and to 25 in 1776, exclusive of the Governor's Foot Guard, organized in 1771. The age limit was reduced to 45 in 1772; the colony was getting where it no longer needed the service of old men in the field. In 1773 the number of enrolled militia was 26,260, divided into 18 regiments with a troop of horse attached to each and to some two troops. The train bands drilled four days each year and each regiment attended regimental exercises once in four years. Soldiers and householders provided themselves with arms.

On the death of Col. Hall in 1773, Elihu Chauncey became colonel of the Tenth, Elihu Hall lieutenant-colonel, and James Wadsworth, Jr., major. The next year, Col. Chauncey resigning, Wadsworth became colonel, Jonathan Baldwin of Waterbury lieutenant-colonel, and Reuben Atwater major. At this time the Assembly ordered that the men should drill on eleven half-days from October to May, but the order was soon revoked. As a little too strong a spirit of sociability was finding its way into the different regiments, the Assembly passed a law to discourage "the practice of treating or entertaining by persons chosen to office;" such practice should be considered disqualification for further promotion. Just when that law was repealed, if ever, is not known. Those were the days when parades, like town meetings, were "opened" with prayer.

II. The Revolutionary War.

Though there were in Waterbury many members of the Church of England, who by their blind faith were of course Tories, the mass of the people were loyal to America when the states combined to resent the insults and injuries heaped upon them by the mother country. In town meeting, November 17, 1774, they endorsed the association entered into by Congress and appointed a committee to see that the town lived up to the endorsement. January 12, 1775, the town meeting ordered the selectmen to procure a stock of ammunition and to build a store-house for it. By the law of 1741 every town was supposed to have on hand 50 pounds of powder, 200 weight of bullets and 300 flints for every 60 enlisted men.

April 21, 1775, Col. Wadsworth of the Tenth wrote from Wallingford in great haste to Lieut. Col. Baldwin in this town that word had been received from the "Boston government" of a collision between his majesty's troops and the people of the colony, and ordering Col. Baldwin to notify the captains of the different Waterbury companies to have their men in readiness.

Following the skirmishes at Lexington and Concord, the Legislature authorized the formation of six regiments for the field, 100 men in each company. David Wooster was made major-general, Joseph Spencer first brigadier-general and Israel Putnam second brigadier-general. The eighth company of the First regiment was formed in Waterbury with Phineas Porter captain, Stephen Mathews first lieutenant, Isaac Brownson, Jr. second lieutenant and David Smith ensign. The last named rose to the rank of major and afterwards was major-general in this State. Gen. Wooster commanded the regiment. Enlistment was for seven months. Each man should receive 52 shillings and one month's pay in advance, which was 40 shillings, besides 10 shillings for the use of his firearms and sixpence a day for billeting money. This company was sent with the regiment to guard the coast in Fairfield county and then up the Hudson to Lake Champlain.

Waterbury also furnished two officers for the fifth company of this regiment, First Lieut. Jesse Curtis and Second Lieut. Nathaniel Edwards. Benedict Arnold was appointed captain of this company but he did not serve with them. They were present at the siege of Boston. A Waterbury man, Ezekiel Scott, commanded the second company of the Second regiment.

That year the town gave 152 soldiers in all, more than any other town except Farmington and New Haven, and some of them were in nearly all the battles of the army. "No town in the colony, not itself the theater of conflict, made greater personal sacrifices throughout the war than Waterbury."

At home, also, the strife had been of the bitterest kind. Not a few Tory sympathizers did not hesitate to express their views in an aggravating manner. Among them were Capt. Amos Bronson, of the "West" or tenth company of the regiment, and Ensign Samuel Scovill and several men of the same company. Upon memorial of John Sutlief and other Whigs of the company, the Assembly appointed an investigating committee with the result that in May, 1775, the officers were cashiered, and in October the company was disbanded. Capt. Hezekiah Brown, of the tenth company of the regiment, who had been very free in his denunciation of Congress, now openly declared that the Assembly had shown itself as arbitrary as the pope in its dealings with the officers. A committee made formal complaint to the Assembly but no decisive step was taken until the next May, when it was shown that Brown had refused to obey orders to detach men for the service, and he was promptly arrested, tried and cashiered, and the company disbanded. Later he became a captain in the British army, where he died. His real estate, forfeited at the time, was afterward restored to his widow. More than 80 other Royalists joined the British on Long Island, among them Capt. Abraham Hickcox, but most of them were so ill treated that they returned to the government of the States. Many of them succumbed to the hardships to which they were exposed.

Meanwhile, at the beginning of the disaffection, on memorials of Moses Foot and of Joseph Guernsey and others, two new companies had been formed in Waterbury, as the eighteenth and nineteenth companies of the Tenth militia regiment.

When the men returned in December, from the campaign of 1775, Capt. Porter was made major of the Tenth. At this time, it may be said, many held commissions both in the army and in the militia, and sometimes the higher commission was in the army.

The winter was one of continual anxiety and the following summer came a call from Gen. Washington for the militia to drive the enemy from about New York, he hastening on after the evacuation of Boston. Connecticut already had eight continental and nine state regiments in the field but responded at once to the request. The first requisition called out 14 regiments lying west of the river and the second nine lying east of it, to serve till the exigency was over. Raw and undisciplined, the militia proved of little assistance, contributing in no small degree to the panic at Kip's bay, September 15.

Maj. Porter became major of the Fifth battalion of Gen. Wadsworth's brigade, the fourth company of which was from Waterbury, officered as follows : John Lewis, Jr. captain; James Warner, first lieutenant; Michael Bronson, second lieutenant, and Joseph Beach, ensign. In the defense of New York, September 15, Maj. Porter was taken prisoner but was afterwards released, became colonel of the Tenth militia and was transferred to the command of the Twenty-eighth regiment in 1780. Many Waterbury men of the Tenth, with Lieut. Col. Baldwin, joined Washington's army in New York, in August, 1776. Ezekiel Scott was in the same army as captain in the Twenty-second regiment. David Smith as captain and Nehemiah Rice as first lieutenant were serving with Col. Elmore's regiment, in the vicinity of Albany.

Capt. Smith became major of the Eighth "Connecticut Line," sub-inspector of Varnum's brigade at Valley Forge, where he spent the famous winter of 1777-8, and brigadier-major of the Second Connecticut brigade, May 13, 1779. In Col. Heman Swift's battalion, raised for service with Gen. Gates, in the vicinity of Ticonderoga, July to November, 1776, Stephen Matthews of Waterbury commanded the fourth company and Amos Hecock, Jr., was second lieutenant.

July 4, 1776, memorable day, the householders of the place formed an independent company under Jonathan Curtis captain, Timothy Pond lieutenant, and Samuel Scovill ensign, armed themselves and reported for duty. A Waterbury company in Col. Thadeus Cook's Second battalion of volunteers, raised in November, 1776, to serve till March 15, 1777, was officered by Benjamin Richards captain, Isaac Bronson, Jr. first lieutenant, William Law second lieutenant, Benjamin Fenn, Jr. ensign.

Near the close of that year, the Assembly formed the militia, 23,000 men, into two divisions, six brigades, 24 regiments, (all male persons between 16 and 60, with certain exceptions) to serve in case of alarm. This is the first appearance of the division and brigade formation. David Wooster and Jabez Huntington were major-generals; Eliphalet Dyer, Gurdon Saltonstall, Oliver Wolcott, Erastus Wolcott, James Wadsworth and Gold S. Silliman, brigadier-generals; Charles Wolf, P. B. Bradley, Jedidiah Huntington, Fisher Gay, Comfort Sage, John Douglas and Samuel Selden, William Douglas and John Chester, colonels. The officers of Waterbury's companies were: 1, Capt. Phineas Castle, Lieut. Ashbel Porter; 2, Capt. John Woodruff, Lieut. Thomas Dutton; 3, Capt. Isaac Bronson, Lieut. Aaron Benedict; 4, Capt. Jotham Curtis, Lieut. Timothy Pond; 5, Capt. Stephen Seymour, Lieut. Daniel Sanford; 6, Capt. Josiah Terrel, Lieut. Stephen Hopkins.

The Legislature now ordered eight regiments to serve during the war, Waterbury's quota of which was 131 men. The officers under this call were Capt. David Smith and Lieut. Michael Bronson. The town voted bounties of 12 pounds a year and a fund for the families of the soldiers. In addition it was called upon to provide clothing for the men themselves. Material was wanting. At the beginning of the war, blue had been adopted for the regimental colors but as it was not to be had green was substituted. All thought of color for anything was now forgotten in the desire to get cloth. Such was the scarcity that the general could not order uniforms but he urged the use of "hunting shirts, with long breeches of the same cloth, made gaiter fashion about the legs." It was thought such a costume, while being suitable for all seasons, would impress the enemy with the idea that each man was a marksman. All lead obtainable was melted into bullets.

The quota for the Continental "Line" filling up but slowly, Gov. Trumbull acceded to Gen. Washington's request to send a body of militia in the spring of 1777 to serve six weeks at Peekskill, where Gen. MacDougall was then posted. Three regiments were ordered. Jesse Curtis and Amos Barnes were captains in Col. Hooker's command. Taking advantage of this weakening, Gen. Tryon made his attack upon Danbury in April. Among the Waterbury men who went to assist in driving him back was Aner Bradley, who was wounded in the side.

During the summer of this year more militia was called out for the guarding of the Highlands on the Hudson. Of the 25 companies under command of Lieut.-Col. Baldwin on this brief expedition, 12 (numbering only 193 men) were commanded by Waterbury officers. They were Capts. Benjamin Richards, Samuel Bronson, John Woodruff, Phineas Castle, John Lewis, Jesse Curtis, Thomas Fenn, Nathaniel Barnes, Josiah Terrell, Jotham Curtis, and Joseph Garnsey and Lieut. Aaron Benedict. Lucius Tuttle was an ensign. Among the men with Gen. Gates, at the capture of Gen.

Burgoyne, was Lieut. Michael Bronson, who distinguished himself as adjutant of Col. Cook's regiment.

In 1778 the military companies of Waterbury were formed into a distinct regiment under the name of the Twenty-eighth. Phineas Porter was colonel, Benjamin Richards (Westbury) lieutenant-colonel, and Jesse Curtis (Northbury) major. One of the Waterbury companies was known as the " Ringbone."

In each succeeding year the demands for more men to carry on the war were met, but, although only a few at a time were called for, it is difficult for us to comprehend how hard it was to find them. Pay, food and clothing were insufficient. Each town meeting, regular or special, appointed committees to see that Waterbury's quota was kept filled and also to make sure that the levies for food and raiment for the army were met. If a man refused to pay the high taxes, he was assessed double the amount. Not only was the town obliged to guarantee to the soldiers the wages from the State, but also to eke out the amount in later days in order to furnish an inducement, small confidence being placed in the promises to pay on the part of Congress.

As the sea coast was under the control of the enemy, the road passing through Waterbury east and west was the most important thoroughfare connecting New England with the other states. Consequently it was frequently traversed by the different armies with their wagon trains. When the small-pox broke out among the soldiers it spread so rapidly in the vicinity that it was necessary to grant to the citizens liberty to inoculate. In April 1784, Dr. Abel Bronson established a pest-house in Middlebury.

After the capture of Burgoyne, a detachment of the army pitched their tents for a night in the Manhan meadows. On different occasions Gen. Washington and Gen. Lafayette passed through here once and perhaps twice. It was probably in 1778 that Lafayette stopped at Capt. Isaac Bronson's tavern at Breakneck (Middlebury.) He also spent one night at Joseph Hopkins's. It may have been in

1780 that Washington, accompanied by Gen. Knox and an escort, dined at the same place. Tradition has it that he was here again at a later date.

The population of the whole town in 1774 was 3,526, and its grand list £39,826. In 1790 the population of Waterbury was 2,937 and of Watertown, which had been set off from it, 3,170; total, 6,107. Waterbury's grand list was £19,797.

Connecticut had contributed more men for the war than any other State, except Massachusetts, the number being 31,939. In general orders in 1782, Washington spoke of the Connecticut brigade as "composed of as fine a body of men as any in the army," and he called for a review of the men, after which he gave the highest honor to the Second brigade of the State, the only command that ever won such praise from him.

III. The Twenty-Sixth Regiment.

It is frequently stated that the first military organization in Waterbury after the Revolutionary war was in 1793. The fact is that, from the close of the war down to the reorganization in 1816, there were companies (or officers) enough in the original Waterbury district to make up almost the whole of the Twenty-sixth regiment of the Second brigade, First division, while the old Tenth of the same brigade still retained some members here, Samuel Camp, captain in the Revolutionary war, being lieutenant-colonel in 1790. Watertown was set off in 1780, Plymouth in 1795, Wolcott in 1796, Oxford in 1798 and Middlebury in 1807. (Prospect became a separate town in 1827 and Naugatuck in 1844.) There is abundant reason, then, for inserting the names of all the officers of the Twenty-sixth regiment down to 1816, in the list of commissioned officers at the end of this book, the exact dwelling places of most of them, under the new boundaries, being quite changeable and uncertain. They are all "Waterbury" names, familiar even to this generation. It will be observed that many of the officers attained to high rank. It is also noticeable in the records of those days, that most of the representatives and leading men were officers in the regiment. There is no question but that they were earnest men.

In 1793, Lieut. Col. David Smith had risen to the rank of brigadier-general, commanding the Eighth brigade, Fourth division, to which the Twenty-sixth now belonged, and Maj. Aner Bradley was lieutenant-colonel with William Leavenworth (2d) major, and Isaac Bronson paymaster. In the summer of that year, still another company was formed with Noah Baldwin as captain. The Tenth was assigned to the Second brigade, Second division.

As in colonial days, all able-bodied men were subject to bear arms and constituted the active militia, the regularly drilled companies being the "trained" or "train bands." The state officers consisted of a captain-general, lieutenant-general and a brigadier-general, and a brigadier-major to each of the eight brigades. The officers wore blue coats faced with red, lined with white, white underdress, white buttons and blue worsted knot on each shoulder. The men wore "white frocks and overalls." The light infantry men were distinguished by a black feather tipped with red, worn in the hat.

The next year, in addition to the infantry companies, there was a troop of horse, attached to the Eighth regiment of the Eighth brigade. It was composed of Waterbury and Watertown men, with Samuel Gunn as captain.

When Washington was once more called to the head of the army by the French alarm, a body of 5,882 Connecticut militia was detached in 1794, for active service if necessary. In 1806, at the time of the English embargo, a detachment of 3,420 was made but was dismissed in 1809. When Bridgeport was threatened in the war of 1812, the Sixth and Eighth brigades were called upon to be in readiness.

IV. The War of 1812.

From the founding of the colony, through the period of the Revolutionary war, there had been no regular uniform for the men, though some had worn "blue trimmed up with red," in addition to the cocked hat, during the war. White frocks and overalls were also not uncommon. After the war, there was a nondescript dress, sometimes called the "national uniform," already described. The weapons had been culverines, pikes, cutlasses and the flint-lock musket. The flint-lock, though superseded by the percussion cap musket some time previous, was not rejected by statute until 1864. Bayonets, at first fastened into the muzzles of the guns and then, in the early part of the eightcenth century, being made detachable, gradually took the place of the pikes. Some carried cartouches with spaces for 16 rounds of ammunition, but the powder-horn and shot pouch were the more generally used even during the Revolution.

From 1811 to 1815, a distinct uniform was prescribed as follows, for the militia: Short blue coats lined with white, faced, collared and cuffed with red ; stiff, stand-up collar ; front corners of coat turned up with red ; white woolen vest ; blue woolen trousers ; all white buttons ; black stock of leather, velvet or woven hair ; round black hat with japanned frontispiece ornamented with a gilt spread eagle and the number of the company and regiment ; black feather with red tip, to rise five inches above the crown of the hat. For this was soon substituted a hat of "common crown," brim turned up on left side to the top of the crown. For the men in active service the uniform was of similar color ; red stand-up collar, corners of skirts turned up and connected with a piece of red cloth in the shape of a diamond, trimmed with blue cord ; helmet of black jerk leather with a strip of bear-skin from the front across the crown to the back ; black feather with red tip and a cockade four inches in diameter made of black feathers.

When the war broke out, John Buckingham was adjutant of the Twenty-sixth, Aner Bradley, Jr., paymaster and J. M. L. Scovill sergeant-major. James Brown commanded one Waterbury company with Edmond Austin as lieutenant and Gideon Platt as ensign. Lemuel Porter, predecessor of Capt. Brown, was major of the regiment the next year.

John Buckingham and Aner Bradley were both commissioned by Gov. John Cotton Smith as captains of companies for the defense of the State, but as only one company was raised the command fell to Buckingham. The whole 3,000 men raised in the State were to be divided into two brigades, under the command of Maj. Gen. Solomon Cowles. The local company was made the eighth company of the First regiment, Lieut. Col. Tim Shepard, later Col. Elihu Sanford, First brigade. The men were from Waterbury, Watertown, Bethlehem and Plymouth, and the full roster is as follows, those marked with an asterisk serving only from August 3 or 13 to September 16 or 20, 1813, and those with a dagger only from September 8 to October 20, 1814, the others serving during both periods :

Captain, John Buckingham.
First Lieutenant, Joseph Bellamy.
Second Lieutenants, James M. L. Scovill,* Sheldon Hotchkiss.†
Ensign, Stevens Shelton.
Sergeants: Eli Thompson, Israel Williams,* Leveret Bishop,* Daniel Benham, Joseph Tuttle.†
Corporals: Lewis Osborn (prom. sergt.), Isaac B. Castle, Benjamin S. Welton,* Norris North.*
Musicians: George Lewis,* Joseph Steel,* John Thompson, Butler Dunbar, Andrew Bradley.

Privates.

William H. Allen,	Primous Bennett,†	Jonathan Bradley,
Orrin Austin,†	Abraham Blackman,	Asa Bronson,
Reuben Bartholomew,	Eldad Bradley,	Augustus Bronson,
Joseph Beebe,*	(prom. corp.),	Augustus Brown,†
Nathan Benjamin,	Isaac Bradley,	Isaac Bronson,†

Privates—continued.

Isaac Brown,*	Leonard Hecock,†	Eaton Samson,*
Ralph Brown,	Chauncy Jerome,	Ransom Saxton,†
Chester F. Buckley,†	Lyman Jerome,*	Stebbins Saxton,
Calvin Burwell,	Isaac Leavenworth,	Asa Scovill,†
Isaac Byington,†	Elisha S. Lewis,*	Joseph Scovill,†
Ezra Canfield,†	George Lewis,*	Abijah C. Stoddard
Asahel Castle,	Ransom Lewis,	Mark Stone,†
Bethel S. Castle,	Horace W. Mather,*	Mark Storme,*
Levi Castle,	Horace Mathews,*	John Upson,
Seth Castle,	Florian Mathews,†	Horatio Upson,
William H. Castle,	Miles Newton,	Peter Vanderbogart,†
Clark Thompson,	(prom. corp.),	Ard Warner,
Loami Fenn,*	Isaac Nichols,†	Arad W. Welton,
Jarvis Fitch,†	Luther Pierpont,	Eri Welton,
Sheldon Gibbs,	Samuel Porter,	Spencer Wickem,*
Reuben Hall,*	Austin Pierpont,	Leonard Wilcox,*
David Hall,	Seabury Pierpont,	Lewis Wirt,*
Sherman Hall,*	Asher Pritchard,	Amos C. Woodruff.†
Lovet Hawley,	Joseph P. Riggs,*	69 Privates.

It was a time of great confusion and much display of feeling. New England states denied the right of the president to call out the militia and put them under command of a federal officer; they declaimed on the inexpediency of the conflict and were inclined to assume toward the government an attitude of supreme independence. In consequence, excitement ran high on the day of the departure of the company from Watertown. But Capt. Buckingham and his men were thoroughly in earnest. People had gathered from far and near to see them off and perchance to drop a few words of suggestion or criticism. When the preparations had been completed, the Rev. Mr. Griswold approached the captain and besought him to march his men to the meeting-house, that the minister might invoke a blessing upon them. The captain consented on one condition, and that was that the minister make no mention of the war, threatening that, if the condition were not complied with, he would immediately order his men out of the sanctuary. It is needless to remark that the invocation was unpartisan in its nature. After the ceremony, the men sallied forth for New London, trusting God to keep their powder dry. These were men whose soundness of judgment and inflexibility of purpose in later years brought to the Naugatuck valley a large part of its industrial wealth.

In 1814, Waterbury men to the number of 15 enlisted in the regular army and served about one year.

During this war a corps known as the "volunteer exempts" was formed. Of the Second regiment of this corps, Frederick Wolcott was colonel and Aner Bradley lieutenant colonel. There was one company in Watertown but none in Waterbury.

Maj. Porter was promoted to the lieutenant colonelcy of the Twenty-sixth in 1815, which in that day was the highest regimental office, and Aaron Benedict became adjutant. Those were the last promotions for Waterbury men under the old regime.

V. The First Flank and Battalion Companies.

The total of the militia in 1813 was 12,582, all active, no "enrollment." There were four divisions, each composed of two brigades and each brigade averaging about 50 companies. Waterbury's contingent belonged to the Eighth brigade, Brig. Gen. Hinman, Fourth division, Maj. Gen. Taylor commanding.

This great body of men being difficult to handle, in the year 1815 there was one of those periodical reorganizations in which relief was sought, generally in vain. The number of regiments was fixed at 25, 10 companies to a regiment, the number of brigades at six and the number of divisions at three, the law to take effect the following year. In each regiment there was a grenadier or light infantry company, later two. There were five regiments of cavalry, each attached to a brigade of infantry, a regiment containing four troops with 14 privates in each. Then there was a brigade of artillery, two regiments of light and two of heavy artillery, and 20 companies of riflemen, each attached to some regiment of infantry. With the cavalry and artillery gradually diminishing, this formation continued till 1847. In the infantry, the light infantry company was designated the flank company and contained 64 privates. Later there were two of them to each regiment. The others were called battalion companies. Uniforms were no longer in vogue.

By this reorganization the distinctively Waterbury company, founded in 1793, became the First Flank company of the Twenty-second regiment, Second brigade, First division, Maj. Gen. Solomon Cowles commanding. A second Waterbury company made the First Battalion company of the regiment. Brig. Gen. John Brainard commanded the brigade and Col. Lemuel Porter the regiment. James Brown was captain of the Flank company, Gideon Platt, Jr., first lieutenant and Samuel Root ensign. Of the Battalion company, Bela Welton was captain, Pliny Sheldon lieutenant and Ransom Scovill ensign. Capt. Brown became lieutenant-colonel the next year and Capt. Welton major, with Ambrose Ives as surgeon.

John Buckingham was appointed colonel of the Second regiment of riflemen, a ·position which he held from 1816 to 1818. There was one company of riflemen in Watertown but none in Waterbury. In 1820 Waterbury was included in the broad district covered by the Fourth cavalry company, and later in the district covered by the First horse artillery, but there were not many members of these organizations here.

The records of the light infantry Flank company for many years are still carefully preserved and were recently presented to Company A, Second, C. N. G., by Aner Bradley, into whose possession they had been given by Lieut. George Prichard. The names of their ·officers and men are so familiar to-day as to best show that those " men of old " are indeed one with us. On Capt. Brown's promotion to the lieutenant-colonelcy, he was succeeded by Samuel Root. The lieutenants were Anson Sperry and Nathaniel R. Morris.

The list of non-commissioned officers, May 1, 1817, was:

Sergeants, Anson Sperry, Enos Warner, Horace Porter, Jesse Scott.

Corporals, Asahel Pritchard, Ransom Gibbs and Samuel Finch.

Fifes, David Gibbs, Harvey Hill.

Drummers, Samuel Cook, Charles Leonard.

Privates.

Augustus A. Terrell,	Lyman Bradley,	Philemon Holt,
Samuel Adams,	James Chatfield,	Joseph Holt,
Luther Allen,	Asahel Clark,	Artemas Hoadley,
Horatio G. Bronson,	Stephen Cowell,	Silas Hotchkiss,
Andrew Bryan,	John Downs,	Isaac Hine,
Anson Bronson,	Selah Frost,	John Hine,
Isaac Bronson,	Van I. Frost,	Horace Hotchkiss,
Jesse Brown,	David Hayden,	Ansel Merrell,

Privates—continued.

Levi M. Marks,	David Perkins,	Daniel Tuttle,
Humphrey Nicols,	Chauncey Root,	Hiram Upson,
Simeon C. Nicols,	Mark Scott,	Erastus Warner,
Garry Nettleton,	L. W. Scott,	Ransom Warner,
Roger Prichard,	Stephen Scovill,	Richard Worthington,
Gaius Prichard,	Amedeus Sperry,	Calvin Burwell.
Chauncey Prindle,	Lamberton Tolles,	

How closely those names were identified with the business interests of the community every student of local history knows.

And those were the days when Napoleon said the time was coming when no cannon could be fired anywhere in the world without the consent of the United States. Oliver Wolcott of Litchfield was captain-general of the Connecticut militia, Jonathan Ingersoll lieutenant-general, and Eben Huntington adjutant-general.

In the following long days of peace there is little to record save the election of officers, of whom a full list is given at the end of this sketch. In 1818, W. R. Hitchcock was adjutant of the Twenty-second. In 1832, Chauncey Root had attained the colonelcy, with Enoch W. Frost major. David B. Hurd worked his way up to the command of the regiment in 1838. Stephen Payne was lieutenant-colonel, L. C. Hall major, A. P. Judd adjutant, Graham Hurd paymaster, the Rev. Jacob L. Clark of Waterbury chaplain and Daniel Porter, Jr., surgeon. The next year Col. Hurd went one step higher and became commander of the Second brigade. Merit Heminway of Watertown commanded the Sixth brigade. E. J. Porter reached the rank of lieutenant-colonel in 1839, Levi Bolster in 1841, and Richard Welton that of colonel in 1844. Edwin C. Birdseye was lieutenant-colonel and O. Ives Martin major. The staff consisted of Lucius P. Bryan, Waterbury, adjutant; Linus Birdseye, quartermaster; A. H. Martin, paymaster; the Rev. A. Darrow, chaplain; Timothy Langdon, surgeon, and A. C. Woodward, surgeon's mate. The next year Elmore E. Downs was paymaster and the Rev. Jacob L. Clark, chaplain. Col. Welton resigned in 1846.

Another seemingly important incident in this period was the order promulgated in 1823 that thenceforth the flank companies should wear uniforms. In contrast with these the other or "battalion" companies were dubbed "Ragtoes;" but in course of time the distinction was nearly if not quite obliterated.

There are two other Waterbury military men whose names should be mentioned here, Maj. Julius J. Backus Kingsbury and Capt. Reuben Holmes, of the regular army, who graduated together from West Point in 1823. Both distinguished themselves in the Black Hawk and other Indian wars. Holmes became a captain of dragoons. He died of cholera near St. Louis in 1853. Kingsbury was promoted captain February 13, 1837, was breveted major in August, 1848, for bravery in the Mexican war, and was appointed major of the First Infantry, May 7, 1849. He was dismissed from the service January 27, 1853, and died in Washington four years later.

At a period when a great change was about to take place, it is worth while to glance back at the military customs of the century up to this date. There were few regular drills by companies, but twice a year the companies and once a year the regiments met for parade and inspection, in the fall and in the spring. The Twenty-second met usually in Cheshire, Meriden or Waterbury, with headquarters at some tavern or inn. Each man must have eight cartridges, blank or weighing an 18th of a pound each, two flints, one priming wire with brushes and one powder horn in addition to the muskets, bayonets, knapsacks, etc. The commissioned and non-commissioned officers held meetings before and after training days, at which time they imposed fines for non-attendance at parades and meetings and transacted routine business. Generally these meetings were held at some tavern, and later, with the company meetings also, at the Tontine Hotel, which was on the south corner of Bank street and Harrison alley and of which Horace Porter was the far-famed proprietor. The customs of the day are indicated by such simple records as these : " Bill for liquors, cake, cheese, pie, crackers, wine and cider, $2; paid." " Liquor bill paid by Silas Hotchkiss and Abner Scott [privates], they having appeared with their evidence to get off their fines." " No bill this evening." " Rum, crackers and cheese, 1 shilling each ; paid."

Training days were the red letter days of the year for the towns in which they were held, not unlike those of the previous century which have already been described. Ministers, magistrates and veterans were invited to the one grand banquet following the "parade," and everyone drank to the health of the guests, never forgetting the clergy. The officers bore the expense in this ratio: Captain 5, lieutenant 4, ensign 3, sergeant 2, corporal 1. The parades became more and more of a farce. The men presented little uniformity of appearance, either in dress or discipline. The names on the book of the First Flank company August 26, 1837, were put down on condition that the dress be made "a plain blue coat, white pantaloons, white vest, and pantaloons to be trimmed with black ribbon three-quarters of an inch wide ; also common black hat with blue plume cockade and tassel, black stock and boots and red belt to go around the shoulder." This costume gave them the nickname of " The Blues."

VI. Following The Flood Wood Period.

With the year 1840 came a touch of discord ; perhaps so long a peace had brought that carelessness which was Cæsar's dread. In the latter '30's the degenerated militia had been termed in ridicule the Flood Woods, a suggestive title for the rag-tag-and-bob-tail that appeared on training days. "The Fantastics" was the title of a motley crowd of men and boys that came out on Fourth of July and on other holidays, to make sport like so many clowns. They were armed with clubs, broomsticks and wooden swords, yet, parading together, it would have been difficult to distinguish between them and the Flood Woods. Discipline was held in contempt.

But up to this time promotion with all its emptiness had been in regular order. This year, however, the members of the Flank company elected as captain one Robert Johnson, Jr., an outsider and almost a stranger. There was little to be said against his military qualities since he had received " a military education in the school at Middletown." But he appeared a veritable martinet to the easy-going Waterbury militiamen and, basing their complaint on the manner of his election, they forthwith proceeded to exercise their innate spirit of independence. Matters were brought to a crisis in May, 1842. This is the last entry in the record book :

"This may certify that the following persons, members of the First Flank company, Twenty-second regiment, appeared near the house of John Sandland in Waterbury, on the first Monday in May, 1842, agreeable to a warning issued by Robert Johnson, then captain of said company. He not appearing the members were inspected by George Prichard, lieutenant of said company, and were found by him to be completely armed and equipped according to law.

"Attest, Charles Scott, Clerk."

George Pritchard, Edward B. Leavenworth, David Welton, Reuben Tyler, Samuel Taylor, Ralph Guilford, Renel F. Sanford, Charles Scott, William N. Russell."

In the very hour of its semi-centennial, the Flank company refused to recognize the authority of its captain. Only a short time before, when it appeared under command of Lieut. Prichard at a celebration in Cheshire, it was said of it: "There is no better military company in the State. Their uniform is of blue broadcloth and silk with gilt buttons made expressly for them."

In 1835, Stephen Payne, who was colonel in 1839, commanded a battalion company in which were many Prospect men. The returns of the company were scanty and it is not known that their records are extant. The officers' names are given in the list at the end of the book.

For light on the chaotic period which followed these days with the final expiring flicker of the First Battalion company, we are indebted largely to the researches of Aner Bradley and to the recollections of some of the veterans of those days. Although there had been some distinguished men among the officers, the existence of the Battalion company on the whole had been rather precarious. Lucius Curtis was the last captain chosen before the election of Richard Welton and the ensuing brief revival. In the summer of 1840, pursuant to the orders of Brig.-Gen. D. B. Hurd, the men assembled on the green to make choice of a commander. They came provided with pitchforks, broom handles and axe helves; blacksmiths with their sleeves rolled up and wearing their aprons, farmers in their roughest dress and every one else, who could spare the time, dressed in working clothes and bent upon having some rare comedy. But Gen. Hurd was on hand, equally determined that there should be some regard for law and order. In voting the men passed through between the sides of the old hay scales which were where the Carrie Welton drinking fountain now stands. For nearly two hours they had their sport, voting for all the incompetent "characters" of the town they could think of. At last, much to his own surprise, Mr. Curtis was elected, to the satisfaction of the general. With the others, he looked upon the matter as a good deal of a joke. Placing him at the head of the procession, the men marched around the town, impressing a farmer's wagon on the way, until they brought up at the Mansion house, kept by Edward S. Chittenden. According to the spirit of the times, Capt. Curtis brought forth pail after pail of rum punch with which the men regaled themselves until, becoming boisterous, they made dire threats against Curtis. At this juncture however, the general interfered, the captain went home in peace and the general retired, remarking that if they had not elected a captain he would have kept them on the green all night.

Capt. Curtis * proved a good man for the position and was enthusiastically assisted in his difficult task by Richard Welton and Henry Merriman who were elected lieutenant and ensign the following year to succeed Arthur Hunt and George Merriman. Capt. Curtis was succeeded by Lieut. Richard Welton. Mr. Welton, a man of considerable property, was perhaps the most popular man in town. His stage route to Meriden was deservedly famous for its splendid equipment and good service. Whatever he put his hand to succeeded. The company had reason to congratulate itself when he took command. But in 1844 Capt. Welton became Col. Welton. Lieut. Merriman, backed by Ensign Charles T. Grilley, kept the command of the company until W. B. Umberfield was elected captain in 1845. Daniel Judd and Henry Smith came in with him as lieutenant and ensign.

September 16, 1845, Col. Welton held a review of the regiment in Waterbury. In its palmiest days it had paraded a good 1000 men but now only 450 responded to the call and after a parade and prayer by Chaplain Jacob L. Clark, the

---

*During the Rebellion he went as a corporal in Company C of the Fourteenth C. V., one of the oldest men in the regiment but determined to help his country in time of need. He was wounded at Antietam and returned home to live to a ripe old age.

men were dismissed for dinner. In the afternoon they were reviewed by Brig.-Gen. F. D. Mills, who bestowed much praise upon the Waterbury company, but more upon that from Meriden. The fact was that, do what they might, interest was waning. Naugatuck having been set off, the population of Waterbury was but 3393 and the young men here as elsewhere had too much pride to have any thing to do with a burlesque such as the militia had become. Col. Welton finding that he had undertaken too great a task in bringing the Twenty-second up to its old standard resigned in 1846. Edwin Birdseye succeeded him and was the last colonel of the regiment. The great change in the militia system of the state took place the following year.

Although Waterbury made no more returns of a company and had no representation in the new Second regiment until 1854 a company was kept up after a fashion under Capt. Umberfield and Capt. Henry Smith with considerable aid from Paymaster Samuel Pritchard who was also called "captain."

VII. The Mexican War.

Since the Mexican war was not one "to enforce the laws of the union, to suppress insurrection" nor "to repel invasion," under the law the militia as such could not be ordered out. Consequently the president made a call for 12 months' troops in 1846. The people of Connecticut having weighed the matter carefully concluded that as yet there was no necessity of their traveling that distance to settle the quarrel and did not respond with even as much alacrity as they did in 1812.

Early in 1847 a New Haven paper said that Charles E. Moss had raised a company of 70 dragoons in this vicinity with the expectation that they would be accepted by the president under the new law. "They are active, stalwart boys and will follow where any man dare lead." The item was copied into the Boston papers much to the amusement of the Waterbury people who had not seen or heard of even the first man who had actually enrolled his name in this company of stalwart dragoons. It was true that Mr. Moss had proffered his services to his country but in general, while entertaining charitable views concerning the war, the people in this section, all parties included, were not inclined to give it a very hearty support. A meeting was called of those in favor of sustaining the action of the government and to condemn the Wilmot proviso. It resulted in a failure, the chairman of the meeting having opened it by declaring his approval of the proviso and his unwavering hostility to the extension of slavery. The "dragoons" were the subject of considerable ridicule, one man describing them thus

"Those seventy hypothetical loons
Called 'Capt. Moss's stalwart dragons.'"

In March 1847, Lieut. Asa A. Stoddard came here and established a recruiting station in Washington hall for the

United States infantry. For a time the uniforms of several who enlisted served as a bait to others but their number was few. Then Capt. Lorenzo Johnson came and obtained 10 recruits for the 10 regiments that were to be in readiness at a moment's notice. Lieut. Stoddard's recruits left for Newport (with the only regiment New England raised) in April whence they sailed May 28 in the steamer North Bend for Vera Cruz to join Gen. Scott's command, reaching there June 26. Charles E. Moss, later a sergeant in the Third dragoons, was one of them. They were assigned to the Ninth regiment to serve under Brig. Gen. Pierce of New Hampshire. The regiment showed great bravery at the storming of Chepultepec, being the first to mount the wall. It was in this war that Maj. Kingsbury won his brevet. Dr. A. N. Bell of Waterbury was a surgeon in the Gulf squadron.

The enlisted men who went from here were: Joseph Grilley (deserted), Lewis E. Grilley (died October 16), Manly Grilley (record of service not shown), Sergt. Edmund B. Gilbert (Goshen), and James Ranger (record of service not shown) all of Company I, Ninth infantry, enlisted March 20, 1847; Henry R. Hatchett, Companies A and B, Ninth infantry, March 17, 1847, died September 17, 1847; Samuel L. Hickox (New Haven) Companies G and I, Ninth infantry, March 20 to December 6, 1847; George F. Hotchkiss (Cheshire), Companies G and I, Ninth infantry, April 19, 1847, to August 21, 1848; Charles E. Moss (Litchfield) Company K, Ninth infantry, transferred to Company E, Third dragoons and promoted sergeant, March 18, 1847 to July 24, 1848; Charles Phelps, Company E, Sixth infantry, March 18, 1847, to July 31, 1848

VIII. Militia Reorganization—Company H.

The militia of the State in 1848 had attained its greatest number, 53,191, of whom 1,704 were riflemen, 1,575 artillery, 508 heavy artillery and 692 cavalry. There were 960 companies divided into six brigades. The condition of affairs throughout the State was practically the same as we have seen in Waterbury. What was everybody's business was nobody's. Realizing the need of a radical change, the General Assembly in 1847 decided to make two classes of all able-bodied males between 18 and 35 (later 45), the active and the inactive or enrolled militia. The commutation or poll tax was fixed at $1 (later $2), which entitled the citizen to exemption from service. Duty for at least three successive days was required of the soldiers, the State to pay them $1.50 a day. There was to be but one division and two brigades, four regiments to each brigade. The First, Third, Fifth and Seventh regiments of Hartford, New London, Tolland and Windham counties respectively formed the First brigade, and the Second, Fourth, Sixth and Eighth of New Haven, Litchfield, Middletown and Fairfield counties the Second. The office of third lieutenant was substituted for that of ensign. All ununiformed and most uniformed infantry companies were disbanded, the Waterbury companies being legally abolished in 1848. The uniform consisted of a dark blue, double-breasted coat edged with white cassimere; turn back and skirt linings of white; silvered buttons; black beaver cap seven and a half inches high with lacquered sunk top seven and a half inches in diameter; a band of black patent leather encircling the bottom of the cap; a black patent leather peak; silver bugle with number of the regiment and surmounted by a gilt eagle; plume of white feathers; chin strap; trousers of sky-blue with white stripes. The Second regiment, Col. Nicholas S. Hallenbeck of New Haven, was made up of companies in this vicinity, including one from Wolcott, but Waterbury had no formal representation. William T. King of Sharon was brigadier-general. Clark Bissell was governor and George P. Shelton of Southbury, adjutant general. The number of companies was again reduced, in 1850, to 99 with 2,904 men and once more in 1852 to 58 companies, 2,045 men.

In actual fact, the State had as yet done little for the militia. The volunteers who succeeded the ridiculous Flood Woods were the very best of material; but, in Connecticut as in the other states, it was to require a Bull Run to demonstrate that zeal and patriotism alone, even when united with Spartan courage, cannot make the soldier. The first bloody disasters of the war and the succeeding long period of delay in active hostilities were due to nothing so much as to the criminal negligence of the states in failing to properly encourage or support their citizen soldiers during the years immediately preceding. As a penalty, thousands of homes to-day mourn the heroes whose bravery, with little other science than that which costly experience taught, preserved the Union.

But the mere reduction of numbers by the law of 1847, coupled with the premonitions of danger ahead in the '50's, had alone served to arouse in the breasts of Waterbury men the spirit which had possessed their forefathers and which had raised so many of them to high positions. While they had held empty titles and idle forms in fitting contempt, earnest organization, though still coming from the people rather than from the State, was attractive to them.

Early in the year 1854 there was a meeting of prominent young men to discuss the formation of a new military company. In May there was talk of organizing a voluntary military company under the auspices of Protector Fire Engine company. "Father" E. B. Cooke of the *American*, always an admirer and promoter of the militia, said in the issue of his paper of May 26, 1854: "No argument is needed from us to urge upon the community the expediency or the importance of sustaining such a corps even for the credit of the city." And then he besought the citizens to help on the cause in a substantial way.

Meanwhile John L. Chatfield and Chandler N. Wayland, as a committee from the meeting of young men, had been soliciting names for a company. Their labors being crowned with success, their petition was duly forwarded to headquarters. Thomas Guyer of South Norwalk was major-general of the State, N. S. Hallenbeck of New Haven was at the head of the Second brigade and Col. John Arnold of New Haven commanded the Second regiment of that brigade to which this company desired to be attached. In the whole State there were 49 companies with 2,467 privates, 1,305 of whom were in the Second brigade.

About September 1, this military "corps" began to assume shape under the name of the American Rifle company with Richard Hunting as captain. A New Haven man, startled by the word "rifle," was led to argue thus for the benefit of the novitiates: "Adopt the musket, either infantry or light infantry, instead of the rifle. The rifle state uniform (blue or green) and the want of bayonets makes a company look insignificant in size and appearance. Besides, the rifle can never be practiced in any infantry regiment as this one is—especially the field movements, and in case of rout, riflemen are not equal to half the number of well-armed musketeers." The musket was the old smooth bore firing buck-shot; the rifle fired a bullet. The rifle was adopted.

The petition of the company having been granted it became Company H of the Second regiment. The special name chosen finally was City guard. The first regular meeting was held September 22, 1854. Wednesday evening, November 1, in the presence of Col. Arnold and Capt. Charles T. Candee of the New Haven "Grays" in Temperance hall, full organization was completed by the election of the following officers: Richard Hunting captain, John L. Chatfield first lieutenant, (recently a lieutenant in the Derby company), Aner Bradley Jr. second lieutenant,

Rufus Leonard, third lieutenant; sergeants, Richard Allen, James M. Colley, James E. Wright, Timothy Guilford; corporals, George W. Cheney, William A. Peck, George Doolittle, Hanford E. Isbell; musicians, C. B. Merrill, Henry Chatfield, Dennis Chatfield. Benjamin P. Chatfield was treasurer, Chandler N. Wayland clerk and Alexander Hine armorer. R. Hunting, Edmund Jordan, B. P. Chatfield, Alexander Hine and Richard Allen had been the committee to secure the drill room. S. G. B. Beales and Marcus Coon were the committee on printing the by-laws. The members elected at a previous meeting, October 4, were Timothy Guilford, Rufus Leonard, F. A. Warner, I. G. Fardon Jr., Henry B. Platt and Aner Bradley Jr. At the next meeting Chauncey B. Webster, Charles Espe, James E. Wright and Lewis Young were taken in. That night, October 13, they had their first experience in drill. At the last meeting before formal organization the new members elected were: John C. Eggleston, Phineas D. Warner and William Scott. Thus the company started out with a goodly number in addition to which there were 40 honorary members who were to pay $5 a year. Expenses were paid by renting the drill room which they had leased, Temperance hall over Benedict & Burnham's store at the corner of Bank street and Harrison alley on the very site of the old Tontine where the light infantry had drilled. The name of the drill room was soon after changed to Military hall.

April 13, 1855, it was voted that the Second brigade should have an encampment in the fall and the question of locality, lying between New Haven and Waterbury, was decided in favor of the latter "because the New Haven and Hartford railroad was not liberal in its dealings with military companies and it was desirable to select a place accessible by other roads." Despite this disadvantage and this decision, however, the encampment was finally held in New Haven. The regiment was then composed of ten companies as follows: New Haven, four infantry and one artillery; Meriden, one infantry; Derby, one infantry;

West Haven, one infantry; Waterbury, one infantry; Birmingham, one rifle. Stephen W. Kellogg was paymaster of the regiment.

May 25, 1855, the company paraded for the first time in uniform. There were 40 odd names on the rolls but only 25 turned out, "many being debarred from equipping themselves for the present in consequence of the disarrangement of the times." With a band they marched through the principal streets and, says the *American*, "their soldier-like bearing was the subject of commendation by all who saw them and, considering the short time the soldiers had for practice and drill, their maneuvering was highly creditable to their improvement." In the forenoon they lunched at the Scovill house and supper was served by Landlord Thayer at the City hotel in the evening.

Companies D and E of New Haven and B of Birmingham were disbanded this year because their members were foreign born which, according to the law, was "inconsistent with the spirit of our institutions." Experience was soon to work an emphatic abolition of such a law.

With a full-fledged military company to help it out, the town now planned a monster Fourth of July celebration. The company, "with new plumes added to its uniform" and headed by Merrill's band, led the procession to a lot on Grove street "at the head of Willow" where there was to be a grand balloon ascension. Though the ascension was a fizzle, the people got enjoyment enough out of the soldiery. August 4 there was a target shoot in the rain which caused the editorial comment, "They are no mere weather troops." And this rain on target-shoot days seems to have become an established thing.

The endeavor was earnest and general to make the militia something more than a party of holiday excursionists. In 1854 the State allowed $100 a year for armory rent to each company. For the following year enrollment was done away with since Congress had voted to make the military appropriation according to the number of representatives and senators instead of according to enrollment. In 1856 the Legislature called the attention of Congress to the fact that the national government still appropriated but $200,000 for arms for all the states, the same as in 1808. The poll tax was 50 cents. That year it was urged that uniforms be made compulsory. Guyer and Arnold being promoted, W. A. Leffingwell of New Haven became colonel of the Second and A. H. Terry of New Haven lieutenant-colonel, Terry succeeding to the command in 1858. A law had been passed ordering a three days' encampment of the officers at Hartford for instruction under Col. W. W. Tompkins of New York. Despite the fact that the Waterbury officers "held an informal meeting in Gilman's saloon to consider the new law," it went into effect and the custom was not abolished by law until the reorganization in 1865. The law also allowed an encampment of from two to three days for each brigade, reduced to one day by act of June 24, 1859.

Camp Ledyard, New Haven, September 5, 6, 7, 1855, was Company H's first camp. Just before this, August 6, Third Lieut. Leonard had resigned and had been succeeded by Sergt Wright. The New Haven *Register* gives us a view of that camp which is not so startlingly different from that of to-day as seen through the lay reporters' eyes: " During the whole of yesterday afternoon and until 11 o'clock, there was a continual procession of vehicles and pedestrians to the camp, and the noise and bustle and the jolly crowds indicated a gala day. The evening passed off without any serious disturbance, owing to the vigilance of the officers and their subordinates who were on the alert to convey offenders to the guard house. And if there were any put there it was no fault of theirs but of the whiskey. We saw no person *intoxicated* but one individual looking down the line of tents inquired which was Chapel street. Many ladies were on the ground to witness the novel spectacle of a military camp and the illumination and were entertained in the *marquee* by Col. Arnold. The weather has been unusually favorable for the parade; the regiment could not have selected two finer days this season. One hundred and twelve tents, each brightly illuminated and spread as they were over large surface, presented a beautiful appearance."

But parade and camp days were not the only ones for outing. Occasionally the most off-hand kind of trips were made to other towns. Thus October 20, the company took Merrill's band and made an excursion to Naugatuck, the rain proving no detriment. Principal A. N. Lewis welcomed them in front of Lane's hotel, they drilled in Nichols hall and on the green, and ended with the usual banquet. It is noted of this occasion that "Col. Welton had charge of the transportation."

The date of the company's conception rather than that of the organization was taken in those days for anniversaries. Without any disparagement of the men who later were to show to the whole world of what stuff they were made, it may be said that they seemed to seek almost any excuse for a banquet. To be a good after-dinner speaker was quite a requisite for a soldier; it was the only inheritance, if such it may be called, from the days of the Flood Woods. And measured by this standard as well as by any other, it must be acknowledged that there was a company full of good soldiers. The laurels they won at those parades and banquets are still green upon the brows of many to-day. They celebrated March 26, 1856, for their second anniversary, parading in the mud in the day time and dining at the Scovill house in the evening, the menu comprising 99 different articles. Apparently the "disarranged times" had come somewhat more into joint. May 1 there was another rain storm and an election parade in New Haven; May 28, more rain, a parade and drill and June 28 the same.

The camp of 1856 was known as Camp Scott and also was at New Haven, August 26, 27 and 28. The officers and men of the brigade numbered 800 of whom nearly half belonged to the Second regiment. There were 250 tents. "Company H was one of the best appearing and one of the most highly eulogized." October 25, Lieut. Chatfield efficiently commanded at the target shoot on Benedict's meadow on South Main street. Lieut. Chatfield won first prize, $12, Priv. W. B. Gibbud second, $9, and Corp. Isbell third $7. On this occasion the company played the host and entertained the Cheshire guard, Capt. Welton commanding, and Mayor John W. Webster presided over the banquet provided by Brown & Dart at the Scovill house.

An epoch in the history of the company and of the town was the election of Lieut. John L. Chatfield to the captaincy March 28, 1857. Capt. Hunting, who had done so much toward organizing the company, and Lieut. Wright both having resigned, Aner Bradley Jr. was elected first lieutenant, Timothy Guilford second and Martin B. Smith third. The sergeants were Marcus Coon, Frank C. Buckland, H. N. Place, F. A. Spencer; corporals, C. F. Church, H. L. Snagg, John W. Hill, H. E. Isbell. On this day the company celebrated its third anniversary. It was reviewed by Mayor John W. Webster and Paymaster Kellogg. The regulation banquet was enjoyed at the Scovill house and the members of the company gave to Capt. Hunting a loaf-cake, also a "beautiful hard-rubber, gold-headed cane," and to Lieut. Wright "a rich pearl-handled knife."

This epoch was followed closely by another, when the still far-off rumblings of war, laughed at by some, were full of portent to others. The women of the city, whose encouragement had already been inspiration for the men, had resolved to give tangible evidence of their interest. To this end they had procured a beautiful silk flag adorned with rich gold trimmings. On one side, in letters of gold, were the words:

| WATERBURY CITY GUARD. |

and on the other,

| PRESENTED BY THE LADIES OF WATERBURY. |

The presentation was made through Dr. P. G. Rockwell after the annual parade May 28, and the occasion was indeed impressive. In responding Ex-Capt. Hunting showed his knowledge of the men who had served under him even as all people should know later, when he said that no stain should ever sully the fair folds of the flag and it never should be surrendered even if its defense meant the knell of the last member. Most sacredly is that flag preserved to-day by the successors of those men whom it inspired to victory.

They turned out July 4 with 30 muskets under the command of Lieut. Bradley and this time the balloon ascension was a success. The Bridgeport Washington Light guard, Maj. Middlebrook, were the guests of the City guard. That year the encampment was in Ansonia for three days from September 16 and it was named after Col. David Humphrey, one of Washington's aids. Col. Leffingwell was at this time in command of the Second.

From that time no public celebration or parade was complete without the presence of the militia, the pride of the town. On the suggestion of Lieut. Aner Bradley, the first general celebration in Waterbury of Washington's birthday was made February 22, 1858, the City guard firing the national salute at sunrise under direction of Marcus Coon, raising the flag on the liberty pole on center square, and giving a parade in the afternoon and a ball in the evening with the never-to-be-omitted supper.

May 4 of that year Lieut. Col. Alfred H. Terry—who was to become the most remarkable volunteer federal officer of the Rebellion—was elected colonel of the Second vice W. A. Leffingwell resigned ; Maj. Ledyard Colburn declining the lieutenant colonelcy, Adjt. J. M. Woodward was chosen. The regiment numbered 325 men.

Hardee's tactics were introduced in August. The first tactics known to the early militia were those of Col. Humphrey Bland, an Englishman, adopted in 1743. These were followed by the "Norfolk Militia Exercise," "ordered by his majesty," in 1764 and continued in general use till 1775. The system of Baron Von Steuben was adopted in 1779. The next change was not made until 1824 when Darrow's tactics were prescribed, to be followed in turn by Scott's, Hardee's, Casey's and Upton's which last named are in vogue to-day in the militia and in the regular army.

May 16, 1858, the company participated in a torch-light parade in celebration of the laying of the first Atlantic cable. Charles Porter's meadow near Holmes, Booth & Haydens' was the scene of the target shoot October 23. Each man was allowed three shots and they riddled the target, Sergt. Place winning the first prize. Returning they saluted at several places with volley firing and then dined at Brown's hotel on invitation of Maj. Partree.

But, as may well be imagined, it was not at all plain sailing for a military company in those days when success depended almost entirely on individual effort with little and uncertain aid from the State. The *American* of February 11, 1859, gives this picture of the times: "When the struggles of this admirable company are taken in view, during the past few years, the time and money expended by its members to keep up its ranks and sustain the honorable standing it has acquired, our citizens might not, cannot look on with indifference in regard to its future prosperity. The very idea of its possible disbandment makes one nervous, and still its slow increase in members does not speak very favorably for the military ardor of Young America hereabouts." But Capt. Chatfield was there and for him there was no such word as fail. February 18 the company gave him a token of their appreciation of his services. That evening was held the fifth annual ball in Hotchkiss hall, Dodworth's quadrille band from New York furnishing the music. There were 200 present and the newspaper says: "Never so brilliant and respectable a ball ever graced that splendid hall." Dinner was served at the Scovill house after which ex-Capt. Hunting, in the name of the company, presented to Capt. Chatfield an

Ames sword of the finest workmanship and in an elegant case.*

At the annual parade on May 30, the company appeared with the latest marvel in the way of firearms—muskets "after the model of 1855 with Maynard's primer attached, bayonets fixed on with a clasp, a light and beautiful piece. It is the only company in the State that has them." First Lieut. Aner Bradley having resigned, Second Lieut. Timothy Guilford was chosen as his successor, First Sergt. Marcus Coon was made lieutenant and H. N. Place first sergeant. As evidence of their esteem for a zeal which had done so much for them, the company presented to Lieut. Bradley a gold-mounted ebony cane. On this occasion Mr. Bradley read an historical sketch of early militia days in this century which was of great value. The interest that had been aroused was never again allowed to flag by the people of Waterbury. During the following winter the company was assisted in procuring uniforms for all the men.

The next annual parade was June 6, 1860. July 4 they went to Bridgeport and captured the town with their fine appearance. In August, the officers of the brigade petitioned for an extra day for the brigade encampment in place of the officers' drill as the parades were not adequate to perfect the requisite discipline. The petition was not granted and camp was ordered at Brewster's park, New Haven, for September 27. The State, by law of 1859, paid for one day's parade but the regiment volunteered another day to get more discipline and to quiet grumblers who said they served for pay.

One of the frolics of the company this fall was the making of a flying visit of one hour and a half, all unheralded, to Birmingham. Incentives to enlist were not so great at that time but that every special attraction was seized upon. At the target shoot that year the first prize was won by Priv. Henry Wadhams of honored memory.

---

* See page 57.

Washington's birthday in 1861 was celebrated with just as much gusto as though the stern reality of war were not right upon them; "there was sound of revelry by night" in Hotchkiss hall, J. G. Jones doing the prompting.

For some time now there had been talk of changing from infantry to artillery and just before the call for troops in 1861, infantry Company H became artillery Company B, making two artillery and seven infantry companies in the regiment.

IX. The Rebellion.

In that eventful year of 1861 Waterbury gave, out of a total of 1609 votes, a majority of 126 against the successful Republican candidate for governor, William A. Buckingham, and for representatives John P. Elton and Israel Holmes, Republicans, were defeated by Green Kendrick and N. J. Welton. The House of Representatives stood, however, 2 to 1 in favor of the Republicans and the Senate 13 Republicans to 8 Democrats. But Waterbury's vote did not mean that she would not do her share to put down the Rebellion as the 900 brave men she sent out attested.

Monday April 15 came President Lincoln's call for troops. Immediately Capt. Chatfield and his men proffered their services and were ordered to rendezvous at New Haven for which place they left April 20 with an almost full quota and what vacancies existed were soon filled. Small sign now of the disbandment or the lack of energy which had sometimes confronted them in time of peace; the appearance of danger meant new life and increased rather than diminished ranks. Such was the spirit of Company B and not once did it flag through the patience-trying period that followed. Everyone wanted to do something. The assistant rector of St. John's church, the Rev. J. M. Willey, added example to precept and, when his offer to go at once as chaplain was not accepted, seized his first opportunity and obtained a like appointment in the Third C. V.

The day the men departed was made a holiday. They were addressed from the band stand on the green by Aner Bradley, now become mayor, the Rev. (afterward Bishop) Hendricken, John W. Webster, S. W. Kellogg, L. W. Coe, C. H. Carter, Dr. P. G. Rockwell, E. B. Cooke and N. J. Buel who, in behalf of the clergy, presented pocket testaments to be distributed among the men, one for each. The Rev. Mr. Willey offered the prayer and the Rev. Mr.

Magill pronounced the benediction. To quote the local chronicler: "All speakers were listened to with most profound attention, the vast audience being as orderly as though in a church. Tears were in many eyes and the very air seemed to be impressed with the solemnity of the scene." Tompkins's and Merrill's bands, consolidated, headed the procession to the station, the fire companies escorting the soldiers. "The streets were jammed; there must have been over 2000 present." A subscription of $1900 was immediately raised at a meeting called to devise means for caring for the families of the volunteers, Mayor Bradley presiding. The special town meeting of April 22 appropriated $10,000 toward the fund. A beautiful American flag was raised over the old Catholic church, 300 Catholic pupils under the direction of the Misses Slater participating in the ceremonies. At a meeting in the basement of the church April 28, T. F. Neville chairman and J. S. Gaffney secretary, 50 volunteered to go. Although no company was then organized and the number of volunteers accepted by the government was considered sufficient, most of them went later in other regiments. At this time Waterbury had $100,000 of government securities and her banks had loaned money to the State. Such was the patriotism of the financiers at a time of great uncertainty in the minds of many. The population of the city was 11,000.

The Waterbury men left here at 3 p. m., April 20, 1861, were assigned to the First regiment and went into camp at Brewster's park, New Haven, as Company D April 22. Capt. Chatfield was at once made major of the regiment and Marcus Coon became captain. Daniel Tyler of Norwich was colonel and George S. Burnham of Hartford lieutenant colonel. The Hartford Rifle company (Joseph R. Hawley, captain), had the right of the line, the Bridgeport Rifles the left.

The full roster of Company D was as follows :

Capt. Marcus Coon ; First Lieut. S. W. Carpenter ; Second Lieut. W. E. Morris.

First Sergt. E. P. Hudson ; sergeants, A. J. Ford, Andrew McClintock, Luman Wadhams.

Corporals, Alfred Carpenter, H. L. Snagg, Jay P. Wilcox, S. L. Williams.

Musicians, G. A. Boughton, Frank Hurlbut.

Privates.

W. Baldwin,	W. F. Gillette,	Fergus Mintie,
G. W. Barnum,	Mason Gray,	David Mix,
A. J. Barnard,	R. G. Hazard,	Philo Mix,
George Beebe,	J. C. Hazely,	Elford Nettleton,
J. A. Blake,	C. N. Herring,	E. H. Norton,
Alexander Bloomfield,	E. J. Hickox,	John O'Neill, Jr.,
David Blodgett,	Arthur Hitchcock,	C. W. Parker,
Frederick Blodgett,	A. S. Hotchkiss,	D. D. Pattell,
J. H. Breckenridge,	Frank Howard,	A. A. Paul,
Arthur Byington,	S. W. Hungerford,	F. C. Peck,
James Callahan,	George Hunt,	Birdsey Pickett,
William Carey,	S. P. Keeler,	S. H. Platt,
Eli Carter,	John Kelley,	Julius Saxe,
Edward Carroll,	John Landigan,	Thos. Smedley,
Henry Castle,	John Lawson,	J. H. Somers,
Patrick Claffee,	Henry Leonard,	E. C. Sterling,
Gustave De Bouge,	J. N. Lewin,	Eugene Sugrue,
Thomas Duffy,	Frank Long,	N. W. Tomlinson,
Redfield Duryee,	F. C. Lord,	C. B. Vaill,
Sebastian Echter,	Augustus Martinson,	George Van Horn,
Fra.ik Edens,	Archb'd McCollum,	Elijah White.
Christ'r Fick,	David Miller,	H. L. Wilson.

The first special honor which the company attained was the being chosen to receive the colors presented to the regiment by Lieut.-Gov. Julius Catlin of Hartford. One man wrote home: "It was an honor to the regiment, but the heart of many a Waterbury boy beat faster, (yes, and for many a day the eyes of Waterbury men, and women too, will glisten when they think of it), when the Waterbury City guard was ordered to advance to receive the colors. It was a proud day—ranked the best among so many noble ones." It may be said here that after the Waterbury men had followed those colors nobly through the Bull Run campaign, being among the few who left that disastrous field in good order, they were nearly deprived of them on their return to New Haven. The captain of a Hartford company sought to take them home with his command, but a determined band of Waterbury men broke into the car and rescued them.

Armed with Sharpe's rifles and Springfield muskets, the regiment left New Haven for Washington May 9, 1861, on the Bienville. Maj. Chatfield, who had received his first promotion from date of muster, April 22, 1861, was promoted to be lieutenant colonel May 10, and then to be colonel of the Third May 31, his soldierly qualities obtaining immediate recognition. It was on August 22 of the same year that he was made colonel of the Sixth.

When Col. Tyler reported with the First, Gen. Scott exclaimed, "Thank God! one regiment has come fully equipped for service." Other men from Waterbury were found in the ranks of the Second and Third C. V. The Hon. James E. English of New Haven, then in Congress, did much for the boys. One instance of his thoughtfulness is particularly worthy of mention here, being recalled by ex-Mayor Bradley. In the confusion following Bull Run, Col. Chatfield's dress uniform went astray with the chest in which it was packed. Word was at once telegraphed to Mayor Bradley to get the uniform duplicated at Hibbard & Snagg's in this city. But next day the order was countermanded. Mr. English had expressed a desire to make good the loss and a few days later, at dress parade, presented a new dress uniform to the colonel.

The three Connecticut regiments were mustered out July 31, but under the call of August 15 for three years' men nearly all re-enlisted in New Haven. Capt. Coon assisted in recruiting Combany B, First squadron, Connecticut cavalry, afterwards attached to the Second New York or Harris Light cavalry, of which Coon became captain. The chaplain of the regiment was Dr. Benjamin W. Stone, formerly of this city.

In 1861 the aggregate of infantry in the militia was 485, cavalry 134 and the total enrollment was 54,968 The Legislature repealing the act governing the militia, all existing companies were disbanded August 1, just when they were most needed. After providing for the enrollment of the inactive militia, it was voted to organize not more than 40 nor less than 64 companies as alarm companies to be apportioned to the several counties according to population. From the inactives enough should be drafted to fill up the ranks. The result was a total of only 13 companies, 385 men, three of the companies from this county. Drafting was tried in vain. The mistake in disbanding the original companies was apparent to all.

But the military ardor in Waterbury did not cool to any appreciable extent. Soon after the departure of the City guard, the Phœnix guard was formed, in May, in Military hall, S. W. Kellogg captain, H. N. Place and E. J. Rice lieutenants, to become Company D of the Fifth, mustered July 23, 1861, for three years. D. B. Hamilton took Lieut. Place's position and Capt. Kellogg remained to assist in organizing the Union guard as a successor to the City guard for a home company. C. E. L. Holmes was made captain and S. W. Kellogg and G. B. Thomas lieutenants. The first of October, this command became Company A, Second Connecticut militia under the State law.

In June of that year James E. Coer organized into the Waterbury Zouaves youths between 17 and 20 years of age. Mr. Coer was captain and A. B. Crook and G. A. Stocking lieutenants. After showing their skill and determination in a voluntary camp in Oakville for three days, they were allowed to carry guns. So rapid was their advancement that in the following January they became light infantry Company D, James F. Simpson, captain, James E. Birrell and Charles D. Hurlburt lieutenants. George Allen orderly sergeant.

Again and again it was necessary to fill up in the ranks of both these companies the vacancies caused by the large number of enlistments, particularly into the Sixth and

Fourteenth. In the summer of 1862, the Union guard was among the first to respond under the call for 600,000 men and left September 3 as nine months' men, Company A, of the Twenty-third, mustered in November 14. Immediately Capt. Holmes was made colonel and was succeeded by Lieut. Thomas and he by Alfred Wells. Lieut. Wells became captain November 14, John A. Woodwaid of Watertown first lieutenant and George W. Tucker second. Private James H. Whiting was destined to become adjutant the next spring. The Zouaves left five days later to become Company H of the same regiment, A. Dwight Hopkins of Naugatuck leaving here as captain, Birrell and Hurlburt as lieutenants. Capt. Simpson had gone as second lieutenant in Company C, Fourteenth, of which S. W. Carpenter of Waterbury was captain and F. J. Seymour first lieutenant.

A beautiful and unique silk flag was presented to the Twenty-Third by Samuel Holmes, cousin of Col. Holmes and formerly of Waterbury. On it were several designs aside from the regulation coat-of-arms—representing Judges' Cave, Charter Oak and the like.

Meanwhile Martin B. Smith had recruited Company E of the Eighth, which left here August 30, 1861, as the third regular volunteer company from this city. H. N. Place was first lieutenant under Capt. Smith and Luman Wadhams second. C. S. Abbott was also very efficient in procuring recruits, his command being Company H of the Twentieth, mustered in September 1, 1862; he was obliged to resign on account of ill health in November. Numerous were the presents which the citizens made to the officers and hearty was the encouragement for every man who donned the blue.

The number of enlistments is all the more remarkable when it is remembered that the total militia enrollment of the town in 1861 was only 982, and in 1862 only 1173, including those with surgeon's exemption certificates. August 25, 1862, the town meeting voted a bounty of $100 to each recruit in the old regiments and an additional $50 to cover the limitation of the State bounty of $50 which expired that day, making a total of $150 for each volunteer; also $100 for each nine-months' volunteer and $6 per month to dependent relatives. Waterbury's quota under the call for 600,000 men—half for three years and half for nine months—was 207. No draft was necessary. Connecticut was the first State to respond and Waterbury about the first town in the State. As an illustration of the zeal and patriotism with which skilled artisans as well as men in all other walks of life left their business to save their country, nearly one-third of the employes of the Waterbury Clock company were to be found in the ranks in the summer of 1862.

And it is not out of place to recall here also that Waterbury lent its wisdom to the councils of the State as well as its bone and sinew to the war. The Hon. Lyman W. Coe represented the district in the Senate and was chairman of the legislative committee to visit the field of Antietam and investigate the condition of the soldiers. Nor was the city's mechanical skill and ingenuity to prove unequal to the great demands made upon them by the nation. Aside from the tons of machinery that were turned out and the hundred and one useful articles that were made up here, Waterbury furnished two-thirds of the brass ornaments worn by the soldiers, an average of one pound to each man in the army.

In July 1863, at the time of the New York draft riots and when all the northern states were very uneasy as to the issue, Gov. Buckingham called for volunteers for three months' service in the State. Waterbury's "alarm" and "home guard" companies had gone to the front one after the other, swelling the number already there until the quota of the town had been exceeded by 108. It was then that S. W. Kellogg, a prosperous lawyer, at the request of John P. Elton and others, raised a company of 100 men in 24 hours and sent to Torrington for Lieut. Col. S. H. Perkins of the Fourteenth, then at home recovering from a wound received at Fredericksburg, to take command of the company. Mr. Kellogg and C. S. Abbott were the lieutenants. The company, designated Company C of the Second battalion, was under the direct orders of the governor. It drilled two hours every afternoon besides maintaining a guard at the armory night and day. The dire threats that had been made to the effect that certain residences should be destroyed and that no men should ever be drafted were soon silenced. Also, to quiet the turbulent feeling, the town voted to pay $300 to each drafted person, the money to be paid to the government and not to the men, and the treasurer was authorized to borrow $30,000 on the credit of the town.

From time to time the bodies of brave men had been brought home for burial and the citizens had indicated their tenderest sympathy for the bereaved families. But the whole town as one family was deeply affected when the gallant Col. Chatfield of the Sixth was brought home mortally wounded July 31, 1863. Struck by a canister-shot in the right thigh at the battle of Pocotalico in 1862, he had recovered sufficiently to rejoin his command in the following April. It was by his own request that he joined in the operations before Charleston. At the battle of Morris Island, he had reluctantly allowed the Fifty-fourth Massachusetts to have the right of the line in the advance on Fort Wagner, in the twilight of July 18. Under the concentrated fire of Forts Wagner and Sumter and the batteries of James Island, the Massachusetts regiment, obliquing, left the Sixth uncovered. Steadily, rapidly they advanced, over the enemy's outer works, never heeding the terrible storm of shrapnel, canister, grape, hand grenades and bullets, through the moat, over the parapet, down to the casemates and bomb proofs, carrying dismay into the breasts of the enemy. The fire slackened, the cry went up that the fort had surrendered. But the remnant of the brave Sixth was standing alone. Col. Chatfield was lying on the parapet with his leg shattered below the knee. Jackson's brigade which had been depended upon to come to the support with fixed bayonets had stopped to return the fire and their opportunity was lost. Perceiving the situation, the rebels charged three times upon the undaunted Connecticut men as though to annihilate them. The color bearer, Sergt. Gustave de Bouge of Waterbury, had fallen shot through the head in the assault, and before the colors could be taken from beneath his dead body, eight other men had fallen upon them, dead or wounded. Then Capt. F. B. Osborn reaching the spot, attempted to pull the flag from the heap of slain. In so doing the banner was torn through the center and only the part attached to the staff was brought home, to be placed eventually with the others in the capitol at Hartford. Among those who helped keep the colors aloft was Col. Chatfield himself who is remembered by his men to-day as the very incarnation of war in that terrible hour. After he had fallen he still encouraged the men to stand their ground in hope of support. And most nobly did they obey, for three long hours, retiring one by one only after all hope had vanished and they were but a handful. Col. Chatfield, fearing that he would be captured, attempted to drag himself from the fort, when a shot struck his right hand in which he had grimly held his sword till that moment. It was the sword which was presented to him by old Company H in 1859. Before he could recover he was carried from the fort by Private Andrew Grogan of Bridgeport, afterwards lieutenant; he saved only the scabbard and belt which are now in the possession of his family. When, on his way to Beaufort for transportation home, he asked after the colors of the regiment and was told that the remnant of them was saved, he exclaimed: "Thank God for that! I am so glad they are safe! Keep them, keep them, as long as there is a thread left."

Physicians, relatives and friends did all in their power for him, but it could not avail. The brave spirit passed away, on the evening of Sunday, August 9.

He was buried in Riverside the following Thursday, with military and Masonic honors. John P. Elton was chairman of the committee of arrangements. All business was suspended, flags were at half mast and military delegations from all parts of the State were present. S. W. Kellogg commanded the escort. The New Haven Grays were under the command of Samuel E. Merwin, Jr. Among those of the army who came to pay tribute to the memory of the hero was Gen. Robert Anderson, the defender of Fort Sumter, and among the civilians was Gov. Buckingham. The pall bearers were Free Masons. The services were held at 2 p. m., at St. John's Episcopal church, of which he was a member. They were conducted by the Rev. Dr. Clark and his assistant, the Rev. Mr. Smith. Chaplain C. T. Woodruff of the Sixth delivered the funeral address after which the cortege proceeded to the cemetery amid the tolling of bells and the booming of minute guns. At the grave the burial service was read by Chaplain Willey of the Third C. V.

During his comparatively brief service, Col. Chatfield had frequently commanded a brigade. A distinguished West Point officer said of him : " Worth in his palmy days could not handle a regiment better." Chaplain John M. Morris, the historian, wrote : " Connecticut sent forth no more accomplished or gallant soldier than he; he must have won high distinction. A modest, fearless, pure hearted, devoted man—his record is that a knight might envy. His deeds and noble sacrifices will live on sun-lit pages and in warm hearts when new generations shall read the imperishable record of the Rebellion and bless those whose heroism saved the nation and freedom from destruction."

The idol of Waterbury's soldiery, it was fitting that his name should be given to the military company which was in reality a continuance at home of the company he had led to the field. A splendid bronze statue, erected by the members of his regiment and by his friends, now marks his resting place at Riverside.

With another summer came the death of three Wadhams brothers, originally from Litchfield, whose name is preserved by Wadhams Post No. 49, Department of Connecticut, G. A. R. Sergt. Edward Wadhams of Company E,

Eighth C. V., aged 29, was killed at Drury's Bluff May 16, 1864. First Lieut. Henry W. Wadhams of Company K, Fourteenth, aged 33, was killed at North Anna May 26, 1864. Capt. Luman Wadhams of Company A, Nineteenth (Second Heavy Artillery), aged 31, was wounded at Cold Harbor June 1 and died June 3. All three enlisted from Waterbury.

The home-coming of the Twenty-third in 1863 was made a great event. Companies A and H reached here Tuesday noon, August 25 and were escorted to Hotchkiss hall, corner of North and East Main streets, Gen. D. B. Hurd acting as marshal assisted by C. N. Wayland, Capt. E. J. Rice, Guernsey S. Parsons and Walter Bowns. The scene of the ovation was one long to be remembered. Mayor Davies and others expressed for the citizens the debt of gratitude the town owed to these men. Col. Holmes had been compelled by ill health to return at an earlier date.

This year witnessed a revival in the spirit of the state militia. In 1862 with Maj. Gen. William H. Russell of New Haven in command of two brigades, 1,017 men, the Legislature had adopted the pay system. S. W. Kellogg, whose zeal gave him the position of major of the Second militia regiment April 8, 1863, was made colonel vice C. T. Candee Sept. 22, 1863. Capt. Samuel E. Merwin, Jr., of New Haven, was promoted to the lieutenant colonelcy and Capt. G. A. Basserman also of New Haven, to the majority. G. W. Tucker was paymaster, P. G. Rockwell surgeon, J. Eaton Smith chaplain and W. W. Hart of Madison quartermaster. Col. Kellogg made Stephen R. Smith of New Haven his adjutant. Col. Guyer was the senior officer of the Second brigade. Horace J. Morse was adjutant general.

A new artillery company was formed in Military hall September 26, with Chandler N. Wayland secretary and a membership of over 60. E. J. Rice was elected captain. October 5, the members of Company A,* Second regiment,

---

* As a militia organization, this company, most of the members of which went with Company A, Twenty-Third C. V., was not disbanded till November 3, 1863.

voted to consolidate with the new company, which took the name of artillery Company A, Second C. S. M., or the Chatfield guard. At about the same time, Company C, Second battalion, Capt. Perkins, was mustered out of the state service and many joined the new company. The other officers of the new company were: F. L. Mintie, first lieutenant and C. F. Church second lieutenant; sergeants, G. W. Tucker, M. L. Scudder Jr., C. R. Welton, L. S. Davis, C. N. Wayland; corporals, H. M. Stocking, F. B. Rice, E. W. Robbins, A. J. Buckland, Carlos Smith, E. T. Smith, C. P. Lindley, C. B. Vaill; secretary, Gilman C. Hill; treasurer, C. N. Wayland; executive committee, E. J. Rice, O. H. Stevens, J. E. Smith, A. S. Chase, A. I. Goodrich; court martial, C. F. Church, G. W. Tucker, M. L. Scudder, H. F. Bassett, W. P. Thomas, E. L. Bronson.

Privates.

C. S. Abbott,
S. J. Allen,
F. L. Allen,
John Adt,
H. F. Bassett,
Truman H. Bartlett,
Walter Bound,
William Burnes,
Aner Bradley, Jr.,
G. H. Benedict,
Alpheus A. Bradley,
Alfred Bluet,
E. L. Bronson,
Mathew Budge,
Alexander Buchanan,
Andrew J. Barnes,
Henry T. Bronson,
George Barnes,
J. S. Bancroft,
John W. Burritt,
Jonathan R. Baldwin,
John J. Blackman,
George E. Bissell,
Wm. D. Cummings,
Calvin H. Carter,
Irving H. Coe,

Elam W. Church,
Augustus S. Chase,
Wm. A. Cargill,
Thomas Coulter,
Samuel H. Cowles,
Edward Croft,
Walter H. Cook,
John J. Davis,
Jesse J. Ford,
John E. Durand,
Richard W. Davis,
Charles A. Darrow,
William H. Davis,
A. Fayette Fisk,
William M. Ford,
Edward A. Fox,
Louis D. Griggs,
Henry C. Griggs,
A. I. Goodrich,
E. H. Gaylord,
Marcus Goudkop,
W. O. Guilford,
Amos M. Geer,
James M. Holmes,
Edward J. Hayden,
Fred'k B. Hoadley,

John W. Hill,
Gilman C. Hill,
Edwin B. Harper,
Addison W. Hagard,
Henry W. Keeler,
Charles Karrmann,
A. N. Lewis,
John D. Lyman,
Reuben S. Morse,
David H. Meloy,
L. I. Munson,
Andrew J. McClintock,
Alexander McNeill,
Henry Overing,
Nelson Parsons,
Edwin Putnam,
H. L. B. Pond,
E. B. Platt,
Dwight F. Peck,
A. Preiss,
Frank M. Rose,
William Renison,
Joseph Srahan,
Mark L. Sperry,
O. H. Stevens,
Peter F. Snagg,

Privates—continued.

John E. Smith,	Henry T. Sanford,	C. B. Webster,
William H. Shepard,	Andrew Storz,	E. D. Welton,
Adam Seibert,	George L. Townsend,	D. S. Weldman,
John Stone,	William P. Thomas,	Alfred Wells,
James Spruce, Jr.,	Henry A. Todd,	Frank Washburn.
A. Skates,	Charles N. Upson,	Thomas Willis,
Lucius Stevens,	Asaph H. Upson,	Martin B. Wedge.
TenEyck D. Snyder,	Allen B. Wilson,	Stephen B. Wedge,
Thos. H. Shurrocks,	Henry B. Winchell,	James H. Whiting.

This list of well known names in itself indicates the high character of the men who were interested. The citizens had raised a fund of $2,500 with which to provide uniforms for the company. John P. Elton was custodian of the fund and an enthusiastic worker in the cause. It seems, however, that no provision had been made for the purchasing of "hats" with this fund and in the end the company were obliged to supply themselves at $30 a dozen. The uniform adopted consisted of light blue trousers and army blue coats.

But before the uniform fund had become available—which was not till the early part of the following year—Company A had seen its first camp, Camp Lyon, Bridgeport, in October. Only the Second and Eighth regiments were there. Company A with Company B formed the First Connecticut Flying battery, a duplicate of the Second Connecticut battery, then in the field.

The names of those of the company who went to the front were borne on the rolls as those of honorary members.

The city's quota under the call of 1863 for 300,000 more was 132. For each new man the bounty amounted to $692 in addition to his pay, and to $792 for each veteran. D. S. Morris was recruiting agent at large, Lieut. E. M. Neville recruiting officer for the First Connecticut cavalry and Corp. D. B. Wooster for the Second Heavies, formerly the Nineteenth C. V. The quota was full before February 1, 1864, at an expense to the town of about $3,000, so that when the call came for 200,000 more, Waterbury was not included in it. The Sixth returned January 21, 1864 and many re-enlisted. The draft of July called for 239 men. The town promptly voted $500 for substitutes, $300 for drafted men or substitutes and $100 for volunteers, in addition to the state bounty of $300. To meet this it was necessary to borrow $100,000. The quota for the call late in this year was 120, which was also filled.

All this was done while the political fever was at its height. It was presidential election year and many were the attacks being made upon President Lincoln, candidate for re-election. In 1862, Waterbury had given 786 votes for Buckingham for governor to 754 for James C. Loomis, the Democratic candidate. In April, 1864, it gave Buckingham, the successful candidate, 728 and O. S. Seymour, Democrat, 809. Green Kendrick, Democrat, was elected senator from this district by 260 and two Democrats from Waterbury, Elisha Leavenworth and Henry A. Matthews, had seats in the House. In November Lincoln received 792 votes for president, McClellan 987. In 1860 Lincoln's vote had been 822, Douglass's 431, Breckinridge's 102 and Bell's 82. In 1864 a guard from Company A was maintained at the armory from the Saturday night preceding till the day after the election. But there was to be little use for it in a community which had given so freely of its men and money.

The militia law was altered again this year, granting $5 each towards the uniforms for the men and allowing four days' encampment. Nevertheless, the roll showed but 1485 active members, not all the towns having followed Waterbury's example. It was eminently fitting that the encampment of the Second regiment, Col. Kellogg commanding, should be held here that year. The time was from September 13 to September 16 and the place the West End meadows, near West Main street, on the banks of the Naugatuck. It was called Camp Chatfield. The regiment numbered 420 officers and men. H. Lynde Harrison was paymaster, George E. Terry sergeant major and Calvin H. Carter commissary sergeant. Tompkins's band now marched at the head of the regiment. Among the interested visitors at the camp were Capt. Alfred Wells and Lieut. John A. Woodward of Company A, Twenty-third, who had just returned from captivity. Col. Kellogg while trying a horse for one of Gen. Russell's staff met with an accident about an hour before going into camp. The horse fell upon him, lacerating the colonel's right leg from the knee to the ankle. He was taken to Surgeon Rockwell's office near the Scovill house where his wounds were dressed, but he was in the saddle again and met the arriving companies at the station, after which he did his work in camp during the four days, but he did not get out of his house again for a week after it.

The work of the women and of individual citizens in behalf of the Sanitary commission through all these troublous years is deserving of an article by itself. Mrs. F. J. Kingsbury was secretary of the first society. In 1865 the citizens gave $1,000, collected by F. B. Merriman, to F. J. Kingsbury, the local treasurer of the commission, as a New Year's present. A society of ladies, of which Miss Jennie Warrilon was president, met regularly at the Y. M. C. A. rooms. In March of that year a fair in Hotchkiss hall netted $1,000 for the Soldiers' home in Hartford.

In April 1865, the town gave Buckingham for governor a majority of 32 over Seymour, Democrat, and elected F. J. Kingsbury and A. S. Chase, Union, for representatives.

Monday April 10, manager C. H. Stancliff took from the wires of the Western Union the message that Lee had surrendered to Grant and the *American* soon had out an extra giving all the particulars obtainable. An impromptu procession was formed, speeches were made and A. B. Wilson, the sewing machine inventor, fired a national salute from a piece of ordnance in his possession. But the Easter Sunday following was turned into a day of deep mourning by the news of the assassination of Lincoln.

At this time Burr Atwood of Nonnewaug, Woodbury, raised a white flag with the words, "The Devil's Dead." When the news reached here, April 19, a party of veterans, militiamen and others, paid Mr. Atwood a visit. He denied having the flag but the sight of a rope so refreshed his memory that the flag was brought forth and came to Waterbury as a trophy. Mr. Atwood, his son and his two daughters were made to take the oath of allegiance and then to unfurl the American flag over their domains. A week later, 75 Woodbury people called on Chauncey Atwood of Nonnewaug, also accused of disloyal sentiments, and he likewise promised to float the stars and stripes thenceforth.' After patriotic speech-making, the party visited Burr Atwood, where they found the country's emblem loyally waving.

The body of Lieut. Col. John Kellogg, U. S. A., late commissary on Gen. Sheridan's staff, arrived here Saturday evening, April 29, on its way to Greenfield, Mass., in charge of his brother, Col. S. W. Kellogg. He died at City Point, April 26. After Company A had escorted the remains from the station, they were placed in Military hall where they lay in state over Sunday.

The mayors of the city during those troublous years were Aner Bradley Jr., always ready for good work, 1861-2-3; L. S. Davies, 1864-5 and John Kendrick 1865-6.

As nearly as can be learned from the existing records in this State and in Washington, the enlistments from Waterbury into the Service were as follows: First C. V. 79; Second C. V. 1; Third C. V. 7; First Squadron cavalry, afterwards Second New York cavalry 8; First Connecticut cavalry 55; First Light battery 2; Second Light battery 2; Third Light battery 5; First Heavy artillery 60; Second Heavy artillery 38; Fifth C. V. 38; Sixth 75; Seventh 22; Eighth 37; Ninth 65; Ninth battalion 11; Tenth C. V. 8; Eleventh 15; Twelfth 12; Thirteenth 13; Thirteenth battalion 7; Fourteenth C. V. 157; Fifteenth 34; Eighteenth 1; Twentieth 66; Twenty-third 71; Twenty-seventh 2; Twenty-ninth 5; Thirtieth (Thirty-first U. S. Colored infantry) 2; Fourteenth U. S. infantry 7; band Harland's brigade, 1; Navy, 30; outside the State, 6.

The grand total is 942. Of course this number includes the men who re-enlisted.

The names and ranks of the commissioned officers who went from this city and the men who won commissions in the field are given at the end of this book.

X. In The Connecticut National Guard.

A new section of light artillery was organized in June 1865 from former members of Company A with some new men. A. B. Wilson was first lieutenant commanding and H. L. B. Pond second. It was known as second section Battery C, Connecticut State Militia, and numbered 30 men, six cannons and 20 horses. The company was not of long duration, attending but one encampment and disbanding soon after.

Thanks to the neglect and carelessness of the State the word militia was still in bad odor although the men who had composed it had made themselves immortal on the field of battle. The material was there; how to utilize it, how to overcome the effect of past mistakes was the question. Listening to the advice of Col. Kellogg the Legislature, by act of July 9, 1865, re-christened the militia the Connecticut National Guard. Other states all over the country have since followed this example. The law was drafted by Col. Kellogg and approved by Gen. Russell and his chief of staff, Francis Wayland, now the head of the Yale law school. By it the eight regiments were made into two brigades—the First, Third, Fifth and Seventh regiments constituting the First brigade, the Second, Sixth and Eighth with the light artillery the Second. The total number of officers and men was 4,141. The law also repealed the officers' annual drill, ordered a six days' encampment by regiment or brigade and provided that uniforms should be furnished by the State. The Second regiment was promptly recruited to ten full companies which number it has had the unique distinction of maintaining ever since.

In September 1865 Chatfield guard changed from artillery to infantry Company A, Second regiment, C. N. G. It numbered 90 men, many of them veterans. The companies of the old Sixth regiment were attached to the Second regiment, making 12 companies besides the battery, over 1,000 men at the camp in New Haven that month, the camp being named after Col. Charles L. Russell of the Tenth C. V. who fell at Roanoke Island. O. H. Stevens was color sergeant of the regiment.

May 2, 1866, Col. Kellogg was promoted to be brigadier general commanding Second brigade. Samuel E. Merwin, Jr. succeeded him as colonel. Not long after, August 12, Capt. E. J. Rice was made major, George W. Tucker succeeding to the command of Company A. George E. Terry was assistant adjutant general on Gen. Kellogg's staff.

The regiment went into Camp Mansfield at Bridgeport that year with a membership of 1,200 against 300 two years before. John P. Elton offered a flag to be known as the Elton flag to be awarded to the best drilled company. After an exciting contest it was won by the Sarsfield guard, Company C, of New Haven. Despite the commendable purpose of Mr. Elton, the contest did not inure to the harmony of the regiment and accordingly the flag was not again put up as a prize. It is still in the possession of Company C.

April 30, 1866, infantry Company D, Sherman guard, was organized, James F. Simpson captain, William L. G. Pritchard first lieutenant and James M. Birrell second lieutenant. In its armory in Gothic hall on Phoenix avenue, it started out with a membership of over 50.

A period of quiet followed the season of unusual activity. The regular routine was broken by an occasional excursion, like that to New Haven in 1867 to do honor to President Johnson, and by the encampments in various places, soon to become an annual event. In 1867 the number of regiments was reduced to four. There were 16 companies and a section of artillery in the Second. It was planned that year to go into Camp Osborn, in West Haven, on a Friday, September 8, but as Gen. Kellogg was opposed to having the men in camp over Sunday, the date was changed to Monday. August 16, 1869, Capt. Tucker was chosen senior major with E. E. Bradley of New Haven colonel, succeeding G. E. Basserman successor to Col. Merwin. S. R. Smith was lieutenant colonel. A. I. Goodrich became captain of Company A.

Company D changed its drill hall to Way's new building on Brook street April 9, 1869. In April 1870, Capt. Gilbert was court martialed for conduct unbecoming an officer and in June he was fined $100 and cashiered. In December, after many ballots, John L. Saxe, a charter member, was elected captain. February 21, 1871, the company moved to Hotchkiss hall.

The year 1871 saw still another great change in the militia. In the summer the Legislature decreed that thereafter there should be but one brigade, it to consist of four regiments, with 10 companies as the maximum, and two sections of artillery, one for the First regiment. The First regiment had eight companies, the Second ten, the Third six and the Fourth eight. Eighty-three should be the maximum number of men for each company, afterward reduced to 67 and now 68. Among the supernumerary officers dis-. charged were Maj.-Gen. James J. McCord, Brig.-Gen. Kellogg, Capt.Terry, his assistant adjutant general, and Capt.H Lynde Harrison, aid-de-camp. Gen. Kellogg had resigned in 1870 after entering Congress but the governor had not accepted his resignation. The new order also disbanded Company D, causing the *American* to remark : " Under the charge of Capt. Saxe and his assistants, Company D had made visible improvement and it seems a pity it should be disbanded. But such is the fate of war."

Lieut. Col. Smith succeeded Col. Bradley. The regiment was now equipped with breech-loading Springfield rifles. The uniform furnished by the State under the law of 1865 was of cheap kind. By the new law the regiments were allowed to choose their own, the State to furnish $25 toward each. The First chose dark blue with red trimmings, light blue trousers, and the Third the same with light blue trimmings. The Second and Fourth chose gray with black and gold trimmings. As the expense was not covered by the State allowance, each company made up the amount out of its own treasury. The coats were cut single-breasted and after the "swallow tail" or West Point style. There were three rows of buttons, with cross belts and epaulettes. The hat was a shako.

July 26, 1871, a meeting was held to form a new company to be known as the "Waterbury Light Guard," its ranks open to all young men irrespective of creed or nationality. In September Maj. C. R. Bannon, who had been instrumental in its formation, received word that the company had been accepted by the State as Company G, Second regiment. The men chose the name of Sedgwick guard in memory of Maj. Gen. Sedgwick, and on September 25 elected C. R. Bannon captain, W. S. Wilson first lieutenant and D. A. Magraw second lieutenant. The other charter members were: First sergeant, Michael E. Dugan; sergeants, Frank P. Reynolds, Patrick F. Ryan, John F. McCormack, Terrence E. Reynolds; corporals, Maurice Culhane, William Kelly, Michael Maher, Patrick Lyman, Matthew Byrnes, Daniel P. Noonan, Michael Mitchell, James Tobin; musicians, James Reed, Terrence H. Farrell. The privates were:

Daniel Bergin,	Patrick Hanon,	John Martin,
Dennis Casey,	Peter F. Hosey,	John McAuliffe,
John Culliton,	John Hayes,	Maurice Noonan,
Daniel Cunningham,	James Houlihan,	Thomas Redding,
Myles Daley,	Timothy B. Jackson,	Frank Reid,
John P. English,	Thomas J. Jackson,	Thomas Russell,
James Eustace,	Michael Keeley,	John White,
Edmond Fitzgerald,	James McGuinnas,	Thomas White.

O'Donovan Rossa was brought here to lecture to raise a fund for the purchase of uniforms. Their drill room for a short time was in Meyer's hall on Scovill street and then in Hotchkiss hall. Everyone took hold with zeal and enthusiasm, making it soon apparent that Waterbury had now another company that was to be a credit to the town.

Since he had said in 1872 that the Connecticut militia was at the head of that of all the states, it was quite proper that the Second should go to the inauguration of President Grant in 1873. After being nearly frozen on a delayed train, they did not arrive in time for the parade. Through the influence of Congressman S. W. Kellogg, however, they were awarded the honor, unprecedented for state troops after the war, of a special review by the president and Gen. Sherman the next day in front of the White House on which occasion the compliments of 1872 for the whole brigade were individualized for the Second regiment. Gen. Upton also saw fit to praise them in warmest terms. There was no encampment this year.

The six days' encampment ordered by the law of 1865 was reduced to four days in 1867. In 1870 the encampment was dispensed with for that year, pending the work of the commission appointed to revise the law. Since that revision there has been a six days' encampment either yearly or once in two years for each regiment except when dispensed with by the commander-in-chief in certain cases where an equivalent of time was given in some other way. Of late years, the whole brigade has gone into camp each year for six days. The law reads " annually or biennially as ordered by the commander-in-chief," and at the session of the General Assembly (biennial) of 1889, it was made "not less than six nor more than eight days." It was felt that so much time was lost in transportation to and from and in getting settled for business that much better results could be obtained if the encampment began Saturday afternoon. But unfortunately the men who devised the change neglected to ask for the necessary increase in appropriation. Adjt. Gen. Embler called on the brigade in 1890 to vote by companies whether they would go without the extra two days' pay (including Sunday) but each man to have his allowance of 30 cents for rations. The officers of the Second voted unanimously for the plan but company votes in other regiments decided the matter in the negative. It is worthy of note so far as the religious side of the question is concerned that the chaplains as well as the officers stated it as their emphatic opinion that, with light camp routine, Sunday would be observed by all the men as strictly as at home and by some of them more strictly.

In the years immediately following the war, the regiments held their encampments at various places in their districts. Later the State leased a ground near the Howard house at Niantic and then the present grounds to the north of them, where the regiments went by twos each year. Under Gov. Waller in 1883, the State purchased those grounds and has been improving them ever since until they are unexcelled in the United States. The location on a low bluff near the Sound at the mouth of the Niantic river is delightful while the well-sodded and level earth with its sandy top soil is always dry. Since that time the whole brigade has gone into camp at the same time each year with results that have been most beneficial.

The centennial year of 1876 will long be remembered by the Waterbury soldiers who were in camp with the Second at Philadelphia a full week, September 1-8. Chaplain A. N. Lewis held services Sunday; Companies G and C went into the city to church. Throughout it was a highly creditable encampment.

The first regular local rifle range was established in Waterville the next year but not much attention was paid to practice until in later years when Maj. F. A. Spencer was inspector and the present range in the meadows southeast of the city became a reality. Since then Waterbury soldiers have stood high in marksmanship, in 1888 Company A winning more badges than any company in the brigade and previous to that its company team having covered itself with glory in many a regimental tournament. It is only within three years that Company G has given much attention to this branch of the service, but it is rapidly overtaking some of the veterans at it. Then there were the excursions to Newark in 1872, to Boston and Providence June 17, 1878, of Company A to New Haven July 4, 1879, of both to Wolcottville to the dedication of the soldiers' monument September 10, 1879, of Company A to the centennial celebration in Watertown June 17, 1880, of Company G to Atlanta, Ga., to be present at the laying of the corner stone of Memorial hall, October 16, 1880, of Company

A to Boston July 4, 1883, of both to New York on Evacuation day, November 26 of the same year, to the dedication of the soldiers' monument in Naugatuck May 30, 1885, to New Haven on Founders' day, April 25, 1888, and to Providence and Newport in June 1889. These with the entertainment given to guests at home are some of the more important events which, with the numerous balls and festivals, made an interest for the men. And on great occasions of state, like the funeral of Gen. Grant and again the funeral of Gen. Smith in New Haven, Waterbury was almost always represented.

In 1875 the companies chose Booth's hall at the corner of Phoenix avenue and East Main streets for their armory.

January 8, 1877, Company A was surprised by the resignation of its efficient commander, A. I. Goodrich. Frederick A. Spencer, who, since he was a sergeant of old Company H, had served in the war, had been first lieutenant of the Second Colorado cavalry and at this time was paymaster of the Second C. N. G., was elected to succeed him. In 1878 he offered the Spencer badge to be shot for by members of the company each year. July 25, 1877, at the time of the railroad riots, originating in Pittsburg, a detail of men from both companies was appointed to remain at the armory in readiness to summon the others if the governor should call for them. Realizing more forcibly than ever the purpose for which the militia was maintained, it was ordered that thereafter fifteen quick strokes on the fire bell should call out both companies. At the time of the hatters' strike in Danbury in 1883, though no regular guard was maintained, the commanders of the companies were ordered to hold their men in readiness.

The old Military hall having been refitted, Company A returned to it, giving a dedication ball April 23, 1879. In December Company G took up quarters again in Irving hall, formerly Hotchkiss hall.

That year the Fifth battalion, colored troops, was attached to the C. N. G.; in 1890 the remaining companies of the battalion became the Separate companies. Waterbury never had a colored company.

In 1881, Waterbury was called upon to furnish another major for the Second and on August 28, P. F. Bannon was elected captain of Company G vice C. R. Bannon promoted. A splendid set of horse equipments attested to the company's appreciation of Maj. Bannon's services.

Then in April 1882, Company A lost Capt. Spencer, who was appointed brigade inspector of rifle practice, with rank of major. Under his command, in 1880, the company had received from the inspecting officer of the First and Second regiments, Lieut. Col. Lewis L. Morgan of New Haven, brigade adjutant, this compliment: "Company A was in all respects the finest appearing company I saw in either regiment; there was nothing to criticise; it was in every way complete." The company presented a very handsome badge to their late captain. About the same time they adopted a company pin. F. R. White succeeded Capt. Spencer.

No halls in the city had been large enough for drill rooms and none was well adapted for the purposes of military companies. Petition had frequently been made that a special armory be provided by the State. In due course of time Architect R. W. Hill, who designed the similar buildings about the State, received the commission to make plans for a brick building for armory purposes alone in this city. The lot chosen by the State was at the south-east corner of Phoenix and Abbott avenues, so situated that the grade of the latter avenue was considerably above the foundation on that side. On December 20, 1883, this building was dedicated with lavish ceremony. Among the guests were Gov. Thomas M. Waller, Adj. Gen. D. N. Couch, Brig. Gen. S. R. Smith and Col. C. P. Graham. On the committees were Maj. Spencer, Maj. E. S. Hayden, paymaster on the brigade staff, Maj. Bannon, Lieut. C. H. French, assistant surgeon on the colonel's staff, Capt. P. F. Bannon, Capt. J. B. Doherty who had succeeded Capt. White in command of Company A; Lieuts. James Horrigan and M. T. Bradley and First Sergt. T. F. Meara of Company G, and Lieuts. C. E. Hall and F. K. Woolworth and First Sergt. F. J. Manville of Company A.

At the time of Col. Chatfield's death in 1863, "a former resident" had broached the subject of a soldiers' monument. Many times in later years the matter had been brought up until at last, largely through the influence of the Rev. Dr. Joseph Anderson of the First Congregational church, it had taken definite shape. By private subscriptions, by donations from the companies, by a Grand Army fair and in one way and another the money had been raised. After a competition, the order for the design for the monument—to cost $35,000—had been awarded to Sculptor George E. Bissell of Poughkeepsie, N. Y., himself, as it happened, a volunteer from Waterbury and a paymaster in the navy. The monument, declared the handsomest of its class it the United States, was erected near the west end of the green and was dedicated October 23, 1884, the entire Second regiment participating in the exercises. September 13, three years later, the companies paraded on the occasion of the dedication of the Chatfield monument, also the work of Mr. Bissell, in Riverside cemetery.

The year 1886 saw one more change in the uniform. It had been decreed that the entire brigade should be clothed alike, the serviceable costume of the regular army to be closely followed. The men of the Second discarded their old gray suits and gaudy belts for dark blue, single breasted coats and light blue trousers, all with white trimmings and a careful avoidance of anything of the tinsel nature.

Feb. 19, 1885, the regiment claimed still another major from Waterbury and this time it was Capt. Doherty of Company A, whose place was taken March 2 by C. E. Hall. Under Capt. Doherty the company had led the entire brigade in percentage of attendance at drills during several seasons. A fine set of horse equipments was the company's token to him of their esteem.

December 13, 1887, the officers of Company A, Capt. L. F. Burpee and Lieuts. C. L. Stocking and F. M. Bronson, offered a handsome gold badge to be awarded to the best drilled man at annual contests at the close of the drill season. Both companies now had finely furnished equipment rooms and parlors in the armory.

Maj. Doherty became colonel July 1, 1889, thus bringing the headquarters to Waterbury. F. T. Lee of New Haven was lieutenant colonel. Col. Doherty's staff was selected as follows: A. M. Dickinson, Waterbury, adjutant and captain; George G. Blakeslee, Waterbury, quartermaster and first lieutenant; William H. Newton, Wallingford, paymaster and first lieutenant; Dr. John M. Benedict, Waterbury, surgeon and major; William G. Daggett, of New Haven, assistant surgeon and first lieutenant; Charles C. Ford, of New Haven, inspector of rifle practice and captain; the Rev. Justin E. Twitchell, D.D., of New Haven, chaplain. Fred W. Miller of Waterbury was drum major.

And then still another major was chosen from Waterbury in the person of Capt. Lucien F. Burpee whose successor in Company A was C. L. Stocking. Maj. Burpee's commission dated from February 3, 1890.

By the character of the officers and their positions in civil life, Waterbury easily demonstrated its ability to preserve the prestige of a regiment which, dating from 1639, proudly lays claim to the honor of being the oldest military organization in America, and the people were not slow in showing their appreciation of the distinction which these men had won for the town. Their first public opportunity was splendidly improved on the occasion of the ball given by the Second Regiment Officers' Association in City hall on the evening of February 6, 1890, a social event which has never been surpassed in this city.

January 10, 1890, Gov. Morgan G. Bulkeley appointed Capt. A. H. Embler of Company D, Second regiment, New Haven, adjutant general vice Barbour whose resignation had resulted from a contest between the First regiment on the one side and Gov. Bulkeley and polo players who wanted the use of the armory on the other. March 1, Col. T. L. Watson of the Fourth was appointed to succeed Charles P. Graham as brigadier general and John P. Kellogg, with rank of captain, was appointed an aid on his staff, May 12. Gen. Graham has brought his case before the Senate, now Democratic in complexion, and it is generally considered a lamentable possibility that Gen. Watson's appointment may not be confirmed as a result of the political spite aroused by the recent elections. The Democrats claim that Luzon B. Morris is elected Governor by a narrow majority; the Republicans hold that ballots were thrown out illegally and that there is no choice by the people. The Senate has sworn in Judge Morris and will have nothing to do with the Republican House, thus leaving Mr. Bulkeley as acting governor but putting a stay to all proceedings, including the making of appropriations. If there is no appropriation there can be no camp.

May 28, 1890, the Waterbury companies participated in the field day maneuvers of the Second which took the form of an attack upon Meriden by the New Haven battalion with the Gatling gun platoon of the regiment under Lieut. Col. Lee and the defense of the city by the Meriden, Middletown, Wallingford and Waterbury companies under Maj. Burpee, Col. Doherty acting as referee. It was the finest and most successful piece of practical work ever undertaken in the Connecticut militia.

A brief word as to the present system of drilling may be of interest to anyone who, years hence, may be looking up the military history and customs of these times. Enlistment is for five years. The drill season is from November 1 to June 1, each company being required to drill each week long enough to make a total of five hours for the month. Special attention is bestowed upon guard duty and skirmish drill. Particular instruction is given to line officers and also to non-commissioned officers who meet regularly for that purpose. After January 1 each year, there is at least one battalion drill a month. In the spring each company in the State is required to devote one day to out-of-door drill and one day in the fall is likewise set apart for target practice. There is also one annual muster and inspection. Late in the summer, the whole brigade, four regiments, goes into camp on the State's grounds at Niantic for a six days' tour of duty. For this duty, as for field day, the State allows $2 a day to each soldier; one "ration" (30 cents) a day for each enlisted man, four rations for line officers, and six rations for colonel, five for lieutenant-colonel and four for major and the commissioned staff. In addition, the colonel has an allowance of $60 a year toward expenses. The State also makes proper allowance for horses and their forage, for mounted officers. On the other hand the State exacts from the soldiers a fine of $5 for each unexcused absence from any of the three roll-calls a day. The uniform worn by the men is furnished by the State; the officers are allowed $10 a year toward theirs. It consists of a dark blue frock coat, with a single row of buttons for the men and a double row for the officers, lighter blue trousers with white stripe and black helmet with brass ornaments and spike. Then there is a plain blue fatigue coat and a forage cap with vizor. In full dress uniform, the officers wear shoulder knots. The guns are of the old style Springfield breech-loading, 45 calibre, extremely antiquated and useless, having been issued in 1870.

The companies also have a civil or club organization, controlled by regularly elected officers. As such organization, they debate all matters relating to the welfare of the company, elect into the body as many members as they see fit and arrange balls and entertainments to keep up the company fund. The entire militia is governed by the State Regulations.

The military poll tax in round numbers amounts to $110,000 a year and, with all its liberality, the State manages to get an average surplus of about $10,000 out of this after paying all the military expenses. In return for its expenditures, the government has at hand, ready at a moment's warning, a body of men whose skill, discipline and equipment are said by the national authorities to be second to those of no volunteers in the Union and to be equalled by but few.

Record in Indian and French Wars.

CLARK, TIMOTHY, 2d Lieut., 1759.
FULFORD, GERSHOM, 2d Lieut., 1755.
HICKCOX, SAMUEL, Capt., 1745.
JUDD, SAMUEL, 1st Lieut., 1762.
LEWIS, ELDAD, Capt., 1762.
HOLMES, REUBEN, Col. Illinois Regt. Black Hawk war, 1852; aid to Gen. Dodge. [Grad. West Point, '23; 2d Lieut. 6th Inf.; Capt. of Dragoons, '63; died '53.]

Revolutionary Record.

[It is to be remembered that nearly all the militia served more or less in the field.]

BALDWIN, JONATHAN, Lieut.-Col. 10th Mil., '75-'78.
BALDWIN, ISAAC, Surgeon (10th?) some time during war.
BALDWIN, SAMUEL, (?) 1st Lieut. 2d Co. 5th Bat., '76.
BARNES, AMOS, Capt. in Hooker's Regt., Apr. 5-20, '77.
BARNES, NATHANIEL, Capt. 10th Mil., '77.
BEACH, JOSEPH, Ens. 4th Co., 5th Bat., '76; Ens. in Hooker's Regt. Apr. 5-20, '77.
BEEBE IRA, Lieut. 10th Mil., '77; Capt. 27th Mil., '78.
BENEDICT, AARON, Lieut. 3rd Wat. Co., '76.
BENHAM, ISAAC, Lieut. com'd'g in 10th Mil., '76.
BRONSON, ISAAC, 2d Lieut., 8th Co., 1st Regt., '75; Capt. 3d Wat. Co., '76; Capt. 27th Mil., '78.
BRONSON, ISAAC JR., 1st Lieut., 2nd Bat., '76.
BRONSON, ISAAC, Surgeon, Sheldon's Dragoons, Nov. 14, '79, to end of war.
BRONSON, MICHAEL, 2nd Lieut., 4th Co., 5th Bat., '76; Acting Adjt., '77.
BRONSON, OZAIS, Ens. in Hooker's Regt., April 9, May 20, '77.
BRONSON, SAMUEL, Ens. 2nd Co. 10th Mil., '76.
CAMP, SAMUEL, Ens. 2d Co., 10th Mil., '75; Capt. in Hooker's Regt., March 29, '77.
CASTLE, PHINEAS. Capt. 1st Wat. Co., 10th Mil., '76.
COLLINS, AUGUSTUS, Maj. 28th Mil., May, '82.
CONANT, ROGER, Ens. 18th Co., 10th Mil., '75.
CURTIS, JESSE, Capt. 10th Mil., '75; 1st Lieut. 5th Co., 1st Regt., May 1-Dec. 10, '75; Capt. in Hooker's Regt., Nov. 5-May 21, '77; Maj. 28th Mil., Jan. '80; Res., '82.

Curtis, Jotham, Capt. 4th Wat. Co., '76; Capt. in 10th Mil., '77.
Curtis, Giles (?) Ens. in 6th line, Jan. 1, '77; Lieut. May 10, '80; Res. Sept. 12, '80.
Curtis, Eli, Sergt.-Maj., 8th line, April 10, '77; Ens., Nov. 17, '77; Lieut. April 21, '78; Res., Dec. 4, '79.
Dutton, Titus, Lieut. in Corps Artificers, Feb. 23, '79.
Dutton, Thomas, Lieut. 2nd Wat. Co., '76.
Edwards, Nathaniel, 2d Lieut. 13th Co., 10th Mil., '75; 2d Lieut. 5th Co., 1st Regt. May 1–Dec. 10, '75; 1st Lieut. in Bradley's Bat. '76; Capt. in Hooker's Regt. '77; Capt. in Provisional Regt. '81.
Fenn, Benjamin, Jr., Ens. 2d Bat., '76.
Fenn, Thomas, Capt. 10th Mil., '77.
Fowler, Noah, Lieut.-Col. Com'd'g 28th Mil., May '82.
Foot, Moses, Lieut. 15th Co. 10th Mil., '75; Capt. 27th Mil., '78.
Garnsey, Joseph, Capt. 10th Mil., '75, '77; Capt. 27th Mil., '78.
Grannis, Enos, Sergt. Sept. 13, '77; Lieut. Corps Artificers, Nov. 12, '79.
Hart, Samuel, Ens. 8th Co. 10th Mil., '76.
Hecock, Amos, Jr., 2d Lieut. 4th Co., Swift's Bat. '76.
Hickox, Amos, Jr., Ens. 19th Co. 10th Mil. '76.
Hickox, Joseph, Capt. 8th Co. 10th Mil., '76.
Hopkins, Stephen, Lieut. 6th Wat. Co. 10th Mil., '76.
Ives, Lazarus, Lieut. in Hooker's Regt. Apr. 5–20, '77.
Law, William, 2d Lieut. 2d Bat., '76.
Leavenworth, Nathan, Surgeon's Mate, Mass. Line, Feb. '80 to end of war.
Lewis, John, Jr., Capt. 4th Co. 5th Bat., '76; Capt. 10th Mil., '77.
Mathews, Stephen, 1st Lieut. 8th Co. 1st Regt., '75; Capt. 4th Co. Swift's Bat., '76.
Merriams, Isaac, Ens. in Hooker's Regt. Apr. 5–20, '77.
Osborne, Lott, Ens. 13th Co. 10th Mil., '76.
Parsons, Simons, Lieut. in Hooker's Regt. March 29–Apr. 23, '77.
Pendleton, Daniel, Capt. Corps Artificers, Aug. 26, '77 to end of war.
Pond, Timothy, Lieut. 4th Wat. Co., '76.
Porter, Ashbel, Lieut. 1st Wat. Co. 10th Mil., '76.
Porter, James, Ens. in Canfield's Regt., West Point., Sept., '81.
Porter, Phineas, Capt. 8th Co. 1st Regt., '75; Maj. 10th Mil., '75; Maj. 5th Bat., June 20, '76; Col. 10th Mil., '77; Col. 28th Mil., Jan. '80.
Potter, Stephen, 2d Lieut. 2d Co. 5th Bat., '76.
Rice, Nehemiah, 1st Lieut. in Elmore's Regt., Apr. 15, '76; Adjt. 8th line, Jan. 1, '77; Capt. 8th and 5th line, Nov. 15, '77; continued, '81.
Richards, Benjamin, Ens. 19th Co. 10th Mil., '75; Lieut. 19th Co. 10th Mil., '76; Capt. 2d Bat., '76; Capt. 10th, '77; Lieut. Col., 28th Mil., Jan. '80; Res. in '82. (?)

ROBERTS, JONATHAN, Lieut. 19th Co., 10th Mil., '75.
SANFORD, DANIEL, Lieut. 5th Wat. Co., 10th Mil., '76.
SCOTT, EZEKIEL, Capt. 2d Co. 2d Regt., May 1–Dec. 10, '75; Capt. 22d Continental, '76.
SCOVILL, SAMUEL, Ens. Wat. Co., '76.
SEYMOUR, STEPHEN, Capt. 5th Wat. Co. 10th Mil., 76; Capt. 27th Mil., '78.
SEYMOUR, JOSHUA, Capt. 27th Mil., '78.
SMITH, DAVID, Ens. 8th Co., 1st Regt. '75; Capt. in Elmore's Regt. Apr. 15, '76; Capt. 8th Regt. '77; Maj. 8th line, Mar. 13, '78; Sub-Inspector Varnum's 1st Conn. Brig., Mar. 29, '78–'81; Brig. Maj. 2d Conn. Brig., May 13, '79; subsequently Maj. Gen. Conn. Militia.
SMITH, MATTHEW, Lieut. in Hooker's Regt., Apr. 12–May 20, '77.
STANLEY, ABRAHAM, Lieut. in Hooker's Regt., Apr. 1–22, '77.
STRICKLAND, SAMUEL, (?) Capt. 27th Mil., '78.
TERRILL, ISRAEL, Ens. 15th Co., 10th Mil., '75.
TERRILL, JOSIAH, Capt. 6th Wat. Co., 10th Mil., '76.
TUTTLE, LUCIUS, Ens. 10th Mil., '77.
TUTTLE, TIMOTHY. Sergt. 8th line, May 24, '77; Ens. June 16, '78; Res., May 12, '79.
WARNER, JAMES, 1st Lieut. 4th Co., 5th Bat., '76; Capt. 27th Mil., '78.
WOODRUFF, JOHN, Capt. 2d Wat. Co., 10th Mil., '76; Capt. 27th Mil., '78.

Record in War of 1812.

BELLAMY, JOSEPH, 1st Lieut., Aug. 3, '13 (?); Sept. 8th, '14; Disc. Oct. 20, '14.
BUCKINGHAM, JOHN, Capt., Aug. 3, '13; Sept. 8th, '14; Disc. Oct. 20, '14.
HOTCHKISS, SHELDON, 2nd Lieut., Sept. 29th, '14; Disc. Oct. 20, '14.
SCOVILL, JAMES M. L., 2nd Lieut., Aug 20, '13; Disc. Sept. 16, '13.

BRADLEY, ANER, Lieut. Col. "Vol. Exempts."

Mexican War.

BELL, A. N., Surg. Gulf Squadron.
KINGSBURY, Julius J. Backus, Brvt. Maj. 1st Inf. U. S. A., Aug. '48; Maj. May 7, '49; Dism. Jan. 27, '53. [Grad. West Point '23; 2nd Lieut. 2nd Inf.; Capt. Feb. 13, '37].

Record in the Rebellion.

ABBOTT, CHARLES S., Capt. Co. H, 20th; Sept. 8, '62; Disc. Nov. 10, '62.
BANNON, CHARLES R., 2nd Lieut. Co. C, 1st H. A., March 12, '62; 1st Lieut. Co. B, Sept. 23, '62; Capt. Co. B, Nov. 19, '64; M. o., Sept. 25, '65; Brvt. Maj., Apr. 9, '65.
BIRRELL, JAMES M., 1st Lieut. Co. H, 23d, Nov. 14, '62; Res. Apr. 6, '63.
BISSELL, GEORGE E., Priv. Co. A, 23d, Aug. 20, '62; Disc. Aug. 31, '63; Assistant Paymaster South Atlantic Squadron to close of war.
BRONSON, NELSON, 1st Sergt. Co. E, 8th, Sept. 25th, '61; 1st Lieut. Co. E, March 18, '62; Disc. Jan. 17, '63; 1st Lieut. Vet. Res. Corps, Aug. 19, '63; Disc. Oct. 15, '66; 2nd Lieut. 42nd U. S. Infantry, July 28th, '66; 1st Lieut. June 8, '74.
BRONSON, JOHN T., Sergt. Co. E, 8th, Sept. 25, '61; 2ud Lieut. April 8th, '62, Res. Oct. 2, '62.
BRONSON, MCKENDRIE W., Sergt. Co. A, 23d, Nov. 14, '62; 1st Sergt. Nov. 25th, '62; Lieut. Co. C, Apr. 9, '63; M. o., Aug. 31, '63.
CARPENTER, SAMUEL W., 1st Lieut. Co. D, 1st, April 22, '61; Capt. Co. C, 14th, Aug. 4, '62; Disc. Nov. 29, '67.
CARROLL, WILLIAM, 2nd Lieut. Co. F, 9th, Oct. 30, '61; Res. Dec. 20, '62.
CHATFIELD, JOHN L., Maj. 1st., April 22, '61; Lieut.-Col., May 10, '61; Col. 3d, May 31, '61; Col. 6th, Aug. 22, '61. Died of wounds Aug. 9, '63.
CLAFFEE, PATRICK T., Priv. Co. D, 1st, April 22, '61. Sergt.-Maj. 9th, Sept. 9, '61; 2d Lieut. Co. C, Feb. 25, '62; 1st Lieut. May 18, '62; Died Oct. 5, '62.
COLTON, JOSEPH, Hosp. Steward, 1st., May 28, '61; Quart.-Mast. 6th, June 25, '63; Disc. Sept. 13, '64.
COON, MARCUS, Capt. Co. D, 1st, April 22, '61; 1st Lieut. Co. B, 1st Squad. Cav. (Co. D, 2d N. Y. Cav.), Aug. 29, '61; Capt. Jan. 15, '62; Dism. Oct. '63.
CUMMINGS, JOSEPH H., 1st Sergt. Co. I, 1st H. A., May 23, '61; 2d Lieut. Co. B, Nov. 6, '61; 1st Lieut., March 1, '62. Died Aug. 28, '64.
DARROW, WILLIAM T., Sergt. Co. D, 5th, July 22, '61; 2d Lieut. Co. D, Nov. 7, '61. Res. May 2, '62.
DOWNS, LEVI B., Priv. Co. I, 1st H. A., May 23, '61; 2d Lieut. Co. C, 107th U. S. Col'd Infantry, July 9, '64; 1st Lieut. Co. B, Dec. 6, '64. Disc. Nov. 22, '63.
DURYEE, REDFIELD, Priv. Co, D, 6th, April 22, '62; Adj. 3d, Sept. 21, '63; Col., Dec. 10, '63. Res. May 29, '64.
ELLIOTT, JAMES P., Priv. Co. I, 1st H. A., June 8, '61; Corp., March 9, '62; 1st Sergt., May 23, '64; 2d Lieut. Co. D, 1st H. A., Dec. 10, '64. M. o. Sept. 25, '65.

FOLEY, JOHN, Capt. Co. F, 9th, Oct. 30, '61. Res. Dec. 20, '62.
HAMILTON, DAVID B., 1st Lieut. Co. D, 5th, July 22, '61; Capt. Co. K, Sept. 13, '62. Disc. Jan. 10, '63.
HAMILTON, WILLIAM,1st Lieut. Co. K, 5th, July 22, '61; Res. Nov. 24, '62.
HITCHCOCK, ARTHUR, Priv. Co. D, 1st, April 22, '61; 2d Lieut. Co. D, 25th U. S. Col'd Infantry, June 5, '65; Disc. Dec. 6, '65.
HOLMES, CHARLES E. L., Col. 23d, Nov. 14, '62; Disc. June 18, '63.
HUDSON, EDWARD P., 1st Sergt. Co. D, 1st, Apr. '22, '61; Capt. Co. E, 6th, Aug. 23, '61; Res. Feb. 19, '64.
HURLBURT, CHARLES D., 2d Lieut. Co. H, 23d, Aug. 14, '62; 1st Lieut. April 16, '63; Disc. Aug. 9, '64.
LARKIN, GEORGE F., Priv. Co. C, 1st H. A., March 11, '62; Corp., April 16, '63; Sergt., May 10, '64; 2d Lieut. Co. H, June 15, '65. M. o., Sept. 25, '65.
LEAVENWORTH, MEL. C., Asst. Surg., 12th, Dec. 31, '61. Died Nov. 16, '62.
MARTINSON, AUGUSTUS, Priv. Co. D, 6th, April 22, '63; 2d Lieut. Co. M, 2d N. Y. Cav., Dec. 10, '62. Killed June 17, '63.
MINTIE, ALEXANDER E., Sergt. Co. H, 20th, Sept. 8th, '62; 2d Lieut. Co. I, Nov. 1, '63; 1st Lieut. Co. C, March 17, '64. Disc. May 3, '65.
MORRIS, WILLIAM E., 2d Lieut. Co. D, 1st, April 22, '61; 1st Lieut. Co. D, 1st Cav., Oct. 8, '61; Capt., Oct. 5, '63; Dism. June 16, '64.
NEVILLE, EDWIN M., 2d Lieut. Co. D, 1st Cav., Feb. 1, '64; 1st Lieut. Co. H, 1st Cav., Feb. 16, '65. Awarded national medal of honor for capture of flag. M. o. Aug. 2, '65.
PECK, HENRY B., Capt. Co. H, 15th, Aug. 25, '62. Died Jan. 30, '63.
PLACE, HENRY N., 1st Lieut. Co. E, 8th, Sept. 25, '61. Res. March 18, '62.
PRATT, HENRY A., Q. M. Sergt. Co. A, 1st H. A, March 19, '62; 2d Lieut. Co. G, March 24, '62; 1st Lieut. Co. H, Feb. 18, '63; Disc. March 18, '65.
PRITCHARD, WILLIAM L. G., Priv. Co. C, 14th, Aug. 1, '62; Corp. Jan. 14, '64; Sergt., March 1, '64; 1st Sergt., Sept. 20, '64; 2d Lieut. Co. B, Feb. 15, '65. M. o. May 31, '65.
RICE, EDWARD J., 2d Lieut. Co. D, 5th, July 22, '61; 1st Lieut. Co. I, Nov. 7, '61; Capt. Co. G, Oct. 14, '62. Res. July 22, '63.
ROCKWELL, PHILO G., Surg. 14th, Aug. 23, '62. Disc. March 8, '63.
SEWARD, SAMUEL H., Corp. Co. I, 14th, Aug. 23, '62; 1st Sergt., Feb. 11, '63; 2d Lieut., June 5, '63; 1st Lieut. Co. H, Oct. 20, '63. Disc. July 8, '64.
SEYMOUR, FREDERICK J., 1st Lieut., Co. C, 14th, Aug. 23, '62; Capt. Co. G, Nov. 12, '62; Disc. Dec. 24, '62.
SIMPSON, JAMES F., 2d Lieut. Co. C, 14th, Aug. 23, '62; 1st Lieut. Co. D, Feb. 4, '63; Capt. Co. C, Oct. 20, '63; Disc. Nov. 16, '64.
SKIDMORE, JOHN R., Priv. Co. D, 1st Cav., Oct. 14, '61; Corp. Nov. 9, '62; Sergt. Jan. 18, '64; Capt. Co. B, Dec. 10, '64; M. o. Aug. 2, '65.
SMITH, MARTIN B., Capt. Co. E, 8th, Sept. 6, '61; Lieut. Col. May 1, '63; Disc. Jan. 13, '65.

SNAGG, HENRY L., Corp. Co. D, 1st, April 22, '61; Sergt. Co. C, 14th, Aug. 4, '62; Sergt. Maj. April 15, '63; 1st Lieut. Co. H, Sept. 1, '63; Capt. Oct. 20, '63; Disc. May 5, '64.

SPENCER, Fred. A., 1st Lieut. 2d Colorado cavalry, May 15, '62; M. o. Sept. 23, '65.

SPRUCE, JAMES, 1st Lieut. Co. I, 20th, Sept. 8, '62; Capt. Co. B, April 8, '65; M. o. June 13, '65.

STOCKING, GEORGE A., 1st. Sergt. Co. C, 14th, Aug. 23, '62; 2d Lieut. Co. D, Nov. 13, '63; 1st Lieut. Co. I, Nov. 18, '64; M. o. May 31, '65.

TITUS, GEORGE, Sergt. Co. C, 5th, July 22, '61; Sergt. Maj. Jan. '63; 2d Lieut. Co. E, 5th, Oct. 16, '63; res. Aug. 4, '64.

TUCKER, GEORGE W., 1st Sergt. Co. A, 23d, Nov. 14, '62; 2d Lieut. Nov. 25, '62; M. o. Aug 13, '63.

WADHAMS, HENRY W., Sergt. Co. C., 14th, Aug. 20, '62; 2d Lieut. Co. D, March 3, '63; 1st Lieut. Co. K, Nov. 13, '63; killed May 26, '64.

WADHAMS, LUMAN W., Sergt. Co. D, 1st, April 22, '61; 2d Lieut. Co. E, 8th, Sept. 6, '61; res. March 18, '62; 1st Lieut. 2d H. A., Aug. 18, '62; Capt. Aug. 24, '63; died of wounds June 3, '64.

WELLS, ALFRED, 2d Lieut. Co. A, 23d, Sept. 1, '62; 1st Lieut. Nov. 14, '62; Capt. Nov. 25, '62; Disc. Aug. 9, '64.

WHITING, JAMES H., Priv. Co. A, 23d, Nov. 14, '62; Adj. April 9, '63; M. o. Aug. 31, '63.

WILCOX, JAY P., Corp. Co. D, 1st, April 22, '61; Sergt. Maj. 6, 'Sept. 21, '61; 2d Lieut. Co. A, 6th, Jan. '62; 1st Lieut. Mar. '62; Capt. Co. B, 6th, Feb. 21, '64; killed May 10, '64.

WILLEY, JUNIUS M., Chaplain 3d, June 14, '61; M. o. Aug. 12, '61.

WOOSTER, WILLIAM H. H., Priv. Co. E, 6th, Feb. 28, '64; 2d Lieut. Co. E, April 8, '64; Q. M. Oct. 31, '64; M. o. Aug. 21, '65.

COMMISSIONED OFFICERS.

Colonial Commanders.

1682 Thomas Judd, Sr., Sergt.
1689 John Stanley, Lieut.
1695 Thomas Judd, Lieut.
1703 Timothy Stanley, Lieut.

Captains.	Lieutenants.	Ensigns.
1715 (Dea.) Thos. Judd,	1716 John Hopkins,	1689 Thomas Judd,
1722 Ephraim Warner,	1722 William Hickcox,	1695 Timothy Stanley,
1727 William Hickcox,	1727 John Bronson,	1715 John Hopkins,
1730 William Judd.	1730 Timothy Hopkins.	1722 John Bronson,
		1727 William Judd,
		1730 Samuel Hickcox.

FIRST COMPANY.

Captains.	Lieutenants.	Ensigns.
1730 William Judd,	1732 Sam'l Hickcox,	1732 John Scovill,
1746 Thomas Heacock,	1740 Thomas Richards,	1740 David Scott,
1754 Thomas Porter,	1746 William Scovill,	1746 Nath'l Arnold,
1757 Timothy Judd,	1754 Obadiah Richards,	1754 John Lewis,
1760 Gideon Hotchkiss. (2nd Co. ?)	1756 John Lewis,	1756 Gideon Hotchkiss,
	1761 Amos Hitchcock,	1757 Edward Scovill,
1761 Edward Scovill,	1763 John Nettleton,	1759 James Smith,
1763 Thomas Richard,	1764 Jonathan Baldwin,	1763 Abel Woodward,
1764 Stephen Upson,	1766 Abel Woodward,	1763 Sam'l Hickcox, Jr.,
1767 Jonathan Baldwin,	1769 Samuel Porter,	1764 Andrew Bronson,
1769 Abel Woodward (West),	1769 Peter Welton (West).	1766 Peter Welton,
		1767 Sam'l Porter,
1770 Ezra Bronson,	1769 BartholomewPond,	1769 Thos. Cole,
1771 Thomas Cole (West).	1770 Ashbel Porter,	1770 Stephen Miles,
	1771 Samuel Curtis,	1771 Benj. Richards,
	1774 Phineas Porter.	1771 Nath'l Barnes, Jr.,
		1772 Phineas Porter,
		1774 Reuben Blakeslee.

SECOND COMPANY.

Captains.	Lieutenants.	Ensigns.
1732 Timothy Hopkins,	1732 Thos. Bronson,	1732 Stephen Upson,
1743 Stephen Upson,	1741 Stephen Upson,	1741 John Judd,
1751 Dan'l Southmayd,	1743 John Judd,	1743 Dan'l Southmayd,
1759 Geo. Nichols,	1759 Josiah Bronson,	1759 Eben'z'r Warner,
1765 Jos. Brownson,	1763 Joseph Bronson,	1763 Wm. Hickcox,
1766 John Welton,	1765 Wm. Hickcox,	1765 Aaron Harrison,
1769 Sam'l Hickcox,	1766 Sam'l Hickcox,	1766 Stephen Welton,
1770 Abr'm Hickcox,	1766 Jesse Leavenworth,	1766 Abrah'm Hickcox,
1774 Mich'l Dayton.	1769 Rich'd Seymour,	1770 Sam'l Brown,
	1770 Hezekiah Brown,	1770 Joseph Warner,
	1772 Sam'l Brown,	1772 Nath'l Richardson,
	1774 Stephen Mathews.	1772 Mich'l Dayton,
		1774 Amos Bronson,
		1774 Isaac Brownson, Jr.

THIRD COMPANY.

Captains.	Lieutenants.	Ensigns.
1740 Thos. Blachley,	1740 John Bronson,	1740 Dan'l Curtis,
1751 John Bronson,	1744 Dan'l Curtis,	1744 John Warner,
1754 Phineas Royce,	1751 Jacob Blakely,	1749 Phineas Royce,
1770 John Lewis,	1754 John Sutlief,	1754 Zachariah Sanford,
1772 Sam'l Porter.	1770 Sam'l Porter,	1770 Amos Osborn,
	1772 Thos. Kincaid,	1773 John Lewis, Jr.
	1773 Amos Osborn.	

NORTHBURY COMPANIES.

Captains.	Lieutenants.	Ensigns.
1765 John Sutlief,	1765 Stephen Seymour,	1764 Stephen Seymour,
1766 Aaron Harrison,	1765 Benj. Upson,	1765 David Blacksley,
1767 Dan'l Potter,	1766 Heman Hall,	1765 Sam'l Curtis, Jr.,
1769 Randall Evans.	1769 Eliphalet Hartshorn,	1766 Josiah Rogers,
		1769 Jude Blakesley,
	1769 Josiah Rogers,	1769 John Allcock.
	1769 Bartholomew Pond	

[For Revolutionary period—see Revolutionary Record.]

Twenty-Sixth Regiment,

4th Div., 8th Brig.*

Lieutenant Colonels com'd't.

1787–93 David Smith,
1793–96 Aner Bradley,
1796–99 Daniel Potter,
1799–03 William Leavenworth,
1803–05 Street Richards,
1805–07 Eleazer Judd,

1807–09 Micah Blakeslee,
1809–13 Garrett Smith,
1813–15 Daniel Mills,
1815 Lemuel Porter,
———
1790–95 Samuel Camp (10th Regt.)

[The Majors and First Majors here given won no higher rank.]

First Majors.

1802 Caleb Hickox,
1803–07 Preserve Carter,

1808–13 Isaac Upson,
1815–16 Allen Bunnel.

Second Majors.

1796–1800 Noah Baldwin,
1812–15 Cyrus Clark,

1816 Ira Hotchkiss.

Adjutants.

1790–95 Samuel Royce,
1795–97 Jesse Hopkins,
1797–01 Linus Fenn,
1803–08 Timothy Richards,

1808–11 Miles Dunbar,
1811–13 John Buckingham,
1814 Aaron Benedict,
1815–16 Lyman Potter.

Chaplains.

1795–03 Uriel Gridley,
1803–06 Israel B. Woodward,

1806–14 Russell Wheeler,
1814–16 Roger Searle.

Quartermasters.

1792–94 (?) Wait Smith,
1794–97 Luke Potter,
1797–03 Noah M. Bronson,
1803–06 Jesse Allcox, Jr.,
1886–10 Hector Smith,

1810–12 H. A. Hylegan,
1812–13 Orlando Porter,
1813–15 Lyman Potter,
1815–16 Chester Hurd.

Paymasters.

1792–95 Isaac Bronson,
1795–96 John Kingsbury,
1796–98 (?) Daniel Stone,
1798–03 Josiah Smith,
1803–05 Joseph Leavenworth,

1805–08 Ebenezer French,
1808–10 Isaac Doolittle,
1810–12 John Buckingham,
1812–14 Aner Bradley,
1814–15 Chester Hurd.

*See page 20.

Surgeons.

1795–(?) Isaac Baldwin,
1801–02 John Elton,
1802–05 Samuel Elton,

1805–11 John Potter,
1811–14 Anson Tuttle,
1814–16 Ambrose Ives.

Surgeon's Mates (not prom).

1801–06 Frederick Leavenworth,
1806–07 Ed. Field.

1816 John B. Johnson.

Captains.

1788 Benjamin Upson,
1788 David Buckingham,
1788 Aaron Fenn,
1788 Ebenezer Porter,
1788 Jacob Fenn,
1788 Charles Upson,
1788 William Leavenworth,
1788 Josiah Seymour,
1790 Timothy Gibbud,
1792 Justus Dayton,
1792 Joel Dunbar,
1792 Uri Doolittle,
1792 Oliver Stoughton,
1792 Eben Smith, Jr.,
1792 Eben Hoadley,
1793 Noah Baldwin,
1795 Titus Darrow,
1795 Herman Munson,
1795 Elisha Frost,
1795 Street Richards,
1795 Caleb Hickox,
1795 Samuel Fenn,
1795 Jared Terrill,
1795 Daniel Smith,
1795 Isaac Judd,
1796 Levi Bronson,
1796 Amos Seymour,
1797 John Kingsbury,
1797 Jesse Hopkins,
1797 Stiles Hotchkiss,
1798 Walter Judd,
1799 Enos Hickox,
1799 Ephraim Tuttle,
1800 Jared Prichard,
1800 Eleazer Judd,

1800 Preserve Carter,
1802 Amzi Tallmadge,
1802 Richard Fenn,
1802 Micah Blakeslee,
1802 John Lewis,
1802 Joseph Twitchell,
1802 Lemuel Harrison,
1802 Joseph Bronson,
1802 Josiah Tyler,
1803 Allen Wells,
1803 Garrett Smith,
1804 Asael Merriam,
1804 Isaac Upson,
1805 Joseph Leavenworth,
1805 James Skilton,
1805 Moses Hall,
1805 Eleazer Scovill,
1805 S. J. Hickox,
1805 Harvey Upson,
1806 Daniel Mills,
1806 Philo Bronson,
1807 Calvin Hoadley,
1807 Landon Loveland,
1808 Lemuel Porter,
1808 Joseph Woodruff,
1808 Harmon Bronson,
1808 David Royce,
1808 Jesse Allcock,
1808 Daniel Eells,
1809 Cyrus Clark,
1809 Silas Porter,
1810 Allyn Bunnel,
1810 Samuel Hickox,
1810 Benjamin DeForest,
1810 Luther Hotchkiss,

Captains—continued.

1810 Hezekiah C. Peck,
1811 Titus Seymour,
1811 Ira Hotchkiss,
1812 James Brown,
1812 Silas Grilley,
1812 Lyman Baldwin,
1812 David Woodward,
1812 Gates Upson,

1812 Asa Fenn,
1813 James Tuttle,
1814 Bela Welton,
1814 Samuel Camp, Jr.,
1814 Sedley Woodward,
1815 Levi Hall,
1815 Miles Hotchkiss,
1815 Ebenezer Abbott.

Lieutenants (not appearing later as Captains).

Ard Welton, Charles Frisbie, Timothy Pond, Jr., Elisha Stephens and Demas Judd, '88; Benjamin Baldwin, '88; David Lewis and Arba Cook,'90; John Adams, J. S. Merriman, Stephen Turner, Elihu Spencer and Ethel Bronson, '92; Jacob Hemingsey, Asa Darrow, Mark Warner, Amos Titus and Ephraim Tuttle, '95; Josiah Terrill, '97; Joseph B. Candee, '98; Japhet Benham, '99; Elijah Nettleton, John Merriman, Richard Warner and Daniel Tyler, 1801; D. R. Merriman, Samuel Pardee, Abraham Hickox and Ebenezer Richardson, '02; H. Bronson, S. J. Thompson and John Norton, '05; Thomas Welton, Eli Beardsley and Selden Shelton,'08; Hezekiah C. Peck, '09; Apollos Warner, '10; Edmond Austin, '12; Gideon Platt, Benjamin Fenn, S. B. Scovill, John O'Brien, Levi Hart and Levi Wooster, '13; Pliny Sheldon, '14; Archibald Miner, Elihu Moulthrop and Stephen Stone, '15.

Ensigns (not appearing later in higher rank.)

Sylvanus Adams, '88 ; Elnathan Thrasher, '90; Miles Newton, Elijah Brown, Ezra Lockwood, Jr., Titus Welton, Samuel Buckingham and Philo Hoadley, '92 ; James Scovill, John Hickox, Titus Hotchkiss and James Merriman, '95 ; Sheldon Scovill, '96 ; Daniel Clark, '97; Asahel Lane and Andrew Osborn, '98; Josiah Tyler, '99 ; Joseph Allcox, '01 ; Seymour Welton, Richard Welton, Jr., Eli Hine and David Tyler, '02; Nathaniel Woodruff and Joel Allcock, '04; Eli Beardslee, Ebenezer Frisbie, Ammi Darrow and Isaac Hopkins, '05; Marcus Bronson, '06 ; Reuben Chatfield, Roderick Stanley, Royce Lewis and Wyllys Terrill, '08; Samuel Horton, '09; Samuel Root, Ansel Porter, John Seymour, Eliel Manu, Harvey Stoddard, Archibald Minor and Archibald Stevens, '13; David Warner, '14; Lyman Dunbar, Riley Allcock, Eli Welton, Jr., John Partree, Jr., Moses Pond, Jr., Lewis Parker and Lamberton Munson, '15. Edward S. Merriman, major of band, '10; J. M. L. Scovill, sergeant-major, '11; Chauncey Garnsey, Jr., drum major, '11.

Twenty-Second Regiment,
1st DIV., 2nd BRIG.

Colonels.	*Lieut.-Colonels.*	*Majors.*
1816–17 Lemuel Porter,	1817–18 James Brown,	1817–18 Bela Welton,
1832–34 Chauncey Root,	1818–25 Bela Welton,	1824–25 Orrin Hotchkiss,
1838–39 David B. Hurd,	1825–26 Marcus Bronson	1828–32 Chauncey Root,
1839–44 Stephen Payne,	1835–38 D. B. Hurd,	1832–38 Enoch W. Frost,
———	1838–39 Stephen Payne,	1841–42 Ozro Collins,
1844–46 Richard Welton,	1839–41 E. J. Porter,	1844–47 O. Ives Martin.
1816–18 John Buckingham, (2d riflemen).	1841–42 Levi Bolster, 1842–44 Ozro Collins.	

Adjutants.

1825–27 David Hayden (junior)
1838–43 A. P. Judd,
1844–47 Lucius P. Bryan.

Surgeons.

1817–19 Ambrose Ives,	1831–39 Daniel Porter.

Paymasters.

1817–18 G. M. Hotchkiss,	1843–44 Samuel Pritchard,
1838–39 Graham Hurd,	1844–47 A. H. Martin.
1839–40 Ozro Collins,	

Quartermasters.

1836–38 Jared Prichard,	1838–39 H. A. Smith.

Chaplains.

1838–44; 45–47 Jacob L. Clark.

FIRST FLANK COMPANY.

Captains.	Lieutenants.	Ensigns.
1816 James Brown,	1816 Gideon Platt, Jr.,	1816 Samuel Root,
1818 Samuel Root,	1818 Anson Sperry,	1817 Anson Sperry,
1819 Anson Sperry,	1819 Enos Warner,	1818 Nath'l R. Morris,
1822 E. P. Root,	1821 E. P. Root,	1819 Enos P. Root,
1824 Chauncey Root,	1822 Chauncey Root,	1821 Chauncey Root,
1829 Lauren Frisbie,	1824 Israel Holmes,	1822 Israel Holmes,
1831 Enoch W. Frost,	1828 Lauren Frisbie,	1824 Lauren Frisbie,
1833 Leonard Prichard,	1829 Enoch W. Frost,	1825 Sam'l J. Holmes,
1834 David B. Hurd,	1832 L. Prichard,	1827 Enoch W. Frost,
1836 Merit Tompkins,	1833 D. B. Hurd,	1829 Carlos Hungerford,
1837 A. P. Judd,	1835 Merit Tompkins,	1830 L. Prichard,
1838 J. W. Finch,	1836 A. P. Judd,	1832 D. B. Hurd,
1839 Levi Bolster,	1837 Gabriel Post,	1833 Merit Tompkins,
1839 E. J. Porter,	1838 E. J. Porter,	1835 Abijah P. Judd,
1840 Robert Johnson.	1839 W. H. Eaves,	1836 J. R. Benham,
	1839 Lucius Beach,	1837 J. W. Finch,
	1840 Geo. Prichard.	1838 Levi Bolster,
		1839 L. S. Beach,
		1839 John Southard,
		1840 John Sandland,
		1840 Ralph H. Guilford.

FIRST BATTALION COMPANY.

Captains.	Lieutenants.	Ensigns.
1816 Bela Welton,	1816 Pliny Sheldon,	1816 Ransom Scovill,
1818 Pliny Sheldon,	1818 Ransom Scovill,	1818 Julius J. B. Kingsbury (one year),
1821 Ransom Scovill,	1821 Edward Scovill,	1821 Isaac Brown,
1823 Marcus Bronson,	1823 Edward Welton,	1823 John S. Kingsbury,
1826 Edward Welton (?),	1826 J. S. Kingsbury,	1826 Hiram Upson,
1827 John S. Kingsbury,	1827 Hiram Upson,	1827 Charles C. Judd,
1830 C. C. Judd,	1830 Sherman A. Hickox,	1830 Philo Brown,
1831 S. A. Hickox,	1831 David A. Sprague,	1831 S. M. Morris,
1836 Jas. C. Wheeler,	1833 Julius J. Bronson,	1832 Elias Beebe,
1838 J. M. Grannis,	1838 John S. Welton,	1836 J. M. Grannis,
1839 J. S. Welton,	1839 Arthur Hunt,	1838 George Jones,
1840 Lucius Curtis,	1841 Richard Welton,	1840 Geo. Merriman,
1842 Richard Welton,	1842 Henry Merriman,	1841 Henry Merriman,
1845 William Umberfield,	1847 Daniel Judd.	1847 Chas. T. Grilley,
[1848 Henry Smith].		1847 Henry Smith.

CAPT. PAYNE'S COMPANY.

Captains.	Lieutenants.	Ensigns.
1835 Stephen Payne,	1835 George Payne,	1835 Henry Hotchkiss,
1838 Geo. Payne,	1838 Henry Hotchkiss,	1838 Elizur Kimball,
1839 Elizur Kimball,	1840 J. Hitchcock,	1839 Daniel Hitchcock,
1844 Ives O. Lewis,	1844 Daniel H. Holt,	1841 John Wallace,
1845 Daniel H. Holt.	1845 Jason Hotchkiss.	1844 Jason Hotchkiss,
		1845 Orrin Hotchkiss.

Second Regiment,

C. S. M., C. N. G.

Colonels.
1863–66 Stephen W. Kellogg,
1889— John B. Doherty.

Lieut.-Colonels.
1887–89 John B. Doherty.

Majors.
1863   S. W. Kellogg,
1866–68 E. J. Rice,
1869–75 G. W. Tucker,
1881–84 C. R. Bannon,
1885–87 J. B. Doherty,
1890— Lucien F. Burpee.

Adjutant.
1889— Arthur M. Dickinson.

Quartermaster.
1889— George G. Blakeslee.

Paymasters.
1855–61 S. W. Kellogg,
1877 Fred A. Spencer,
1878–83 Edward S. Hayden.

Surgeons.
1865–66 Philo G. Rockwell,
1883–87 Charles H. French, asst.,
1888   Carl E. Munger, asst.
1889— John M. Benedict.

Chaplain.
1865–68 J. Eaton Smith.

COMPANY H, SECOND C. S. M.

Captains.
1854 Richard Hunting,
1857 John L. Chatfield.

First Lieutenants.
1854 John L. Chatfield,
1857 Aner Bradley, Jr.,
1859 Timothy Guilford,
1860 Marcus Coon.

Second Lieutenants.
1854 Aner Bradley, Jr.,
1857 Timothy Guilford,
1859 Marcus Coon,
1860 Henry N. Place.

Third Lieutenants.
1854 Rufus Leonard,
1855 James E. Wright,
1857 Martin B. Smith.

UNION GUARD, CO. A, SECOND C. S. M.

1861 C. E. L. Holmes, *Captain.*—S. W. Kellogg, *First Lieutenant;*—G. B. Thomas, *Second Lieutenant.*

COMPANY A, SECOND C. S. M., C. N. G.

Captains.	First Lieutenants.	Second Lieutenants.
1863 E. J. Rice,	1863 F. L. Mintie,	1863 C. F. Church,
1866 G. W. Tucker,	1864 G. W. Tucker,	1864 M. W. Bronson,
1869 A. I. Goodrich,	1866 G. A. Stocking,	1865 Carlos Smith,
1877 F. A. Spencer,	1868 A. I. Goodrich,	M. L. Scudder,
1882 F. R. White,	1869 D. L Dickinson,	1866 H. M. Stocking,
1883 J. B. Doherty,	1871 G. H. Cowell,	1868 L. S. Davis,
1885 C. E. Hall,	1876 C. L. Stocking,	1869 C. B. Vaill,
1886 F. K. Woolworth,	F. H. Smith,	E. B. Harper,
F. L. Blakeley,	1880 F. R. White,	1871 W. Wilson,
1887 L. F. Burpee,	1882 J. B. Doherty,	1874 C. L. Stocking,
1890 C. L. Stocking.	1883 C. E. Hall,	1876 F. H. Smith,
	1885 F. K. Woolworth,	F. R. White,
	1886 F. L. Blakeley,	1880 J. B. Doherty,
	L. F. Burpee,	1882 C. E. Hall,
	1887 C. L. Stocking,	1883 F. K. Woolworth,
	1890 W. E. Moses.	1885 F. J. Manville,
		F. L. Blakeley,
		1886 L. F. Burpee,
		F. M. Bronson,
		1888 W. E. Moses,
		1890 C. W. Burpee.

COMPANY D, SECOND C. N. G.

Captains.	First Lieutenants.	Second Lieutenants.
1866 James F. Simpson,	1866 W. L. G. Pritchard,	1866 James M. Birrell,
1867 E. L. Cook,	J. M. Birrell,	E. L. Cook,
1869 James J. Gilbert,	1867 James J. Gilbert,	1867 J. J. Gilbert,
1870 John L. Saxe.	1868 J. B. Perkins,	William Wilson,
	1869 W. S. Wilson.	B. F. Bronson,
		1869 A. Mosier,

COMPANY G, SECOND C. N. G.

Captains.	First Lieutenants.	Second Lieutenants.
1871 C. R. Bannon,	1871 W. S. Wilson,	1871 D. A. McGraw,
1881 P. F. Bannon,	1874 D. A. McGraw,	1874 M. F. Maher,
1884 C. R. Bannon,	1879 T. H. White,	1879 T. F. White,
1886 A. J. Wolff.	1880 James Horrigan,	James Horrigan,
	1881 J. H. Reid,	1881 J. H. Reid,
	1884 T. F. Meara,	1883 M. T. Bradley,
	1886 K. J. Farrell,	1884 T. F. Meara,
	1887 D. E. Fitzpatrick.	A. J. Wolff,
		1886 K. J. Farrell,
		M. Cooney,
		D. E. Fitzpatrick,
		1887 P. Halpin.

Other Companies.

PHŒNIX GUARD.

1861 S. W. Kellogg, *Captain;*—H. N. Place, *First Lieutenant;*—E. J. Rice, *Second Lieutenant.*

WATERBURY ZOUAVES, CO. D, LIGHT INFANTRY.

1862 James E. Coer, *Captain;* A. B. Crook, *First Lieutenant;* G. A. Stocking, *Second Lieutenant.*

1863 James F. Simpson, *Captain;* James M. Birrell, *First Lieutenant;* C. D. Hurlburt, *Second Lieutenant.*

COMPANY C, SECOND BATTALION.

1863 S. H. Perkins, *Captain;* S. W. Kellogg, *First Lieutenant;* C. S. Abbott, *Second Lieutenant.*

LIGHT ARTILLERY, 2nd SECTION, BATTERY C, C. N. G.

1865 A. B. Wilson, *First Lieutenant;*—H. L. B. Pond, *Second Lieutenant.*

Generals and General Staff Officers.

1793–95	David Smith, Brig.-Gen. 8th Brig.
1795–1800	David Smith, Maj.-Gen. 4th Div.
1800–02	Daniel Potter, Brig.-Gen. 8th Brig.
1839–40	David B. Hurd, Brig.-Gen. 2d Brig.
1866–71	Stephen W. Kellogg, Brig.-Gen. 2d Brig.
1800–02	John Kingsbury, Brig.-Maj. 8th Brig.
1866–67	Philo G. Hurd, Surgeon-Gen.
1866–71	George E. Terry, Asst. Adjt.-Gen. 2d Brig.
1877–79	Guernsey S. Parsons, Aid Gov. Hubbard's Staff.
1882	Fred A. Spencer, Brig. Insp. Rifle Practice.
1884–90	Edward S. Hayden, Brig.-Quart.-Mast.
1890	John P. Kellogg, Aid Brig. Staff.

Roster of Company A, February, 1891.

Captain, Charles L. Stocking. *First Lieutenant*, William E. Moses. *Second Lieutenant*, Charles W. Burpee.

First sergeant, Henry B. Carter;* *quartermaster sergeant*, E. J. Schuyler; *sergeants*, W. H. Claxton, J. W. Fitzpatrick, W. L. Munson, W. A. Goldsmith.

Corporals, E. R. Heebner, J. S. Whiteman, F. H. Spencer, James Geddes, Edwin Hart, W. R. Keaveney, H. C. Cady, E. O. Goss.

Musicians: C. A. Lathrop, W. W. Webster, F. E. Webster.

Privates.

R. E. Bailey,	T. E. Guest,	W. T. McClelland,
H. F. Baker,	C. M. Germann,	E. L. Norvell,
C. E. Baker,	Charles Herman,	G. E. Pettitjean,
W. G. Barton,	R. M. Hulsart,	George Proudman,
W. A. Bigelow,	E. N. Humphrey,	F. Reynolds,
G. A. Blanchard,	C. H. Humphrey,	C. H. Ross,
F. C. Boden,	Clinton Hart,	W. J. Snow,
G. W. Brown,	J. M. Henderson,	N. H. Schwartz,
O. H. Burr,	W. H. Haines,	H. S. Scoville,
W. G. Christian,	F. W. Ingraham,	C. W. Smith,
A. Chadwick,	R. Kiersted,	A. N. Trott,
T. Chadwick,	J. E. Marsh,	Charles J. Terrell,
E. S. Carter,	B. W. McDonald,	Robert Walker,
F. B. Daniels,	John McKeever,	J. W. Ward,
H. L. Daniels,	W. H. J. McNeil,	Frank Welton,
E. E. Dewitt,	David Miller,	H. A. West.
John H. Goss,		

---

* Appointed sergeant major March 9, 1891.

Roster of Company G, February, 1891.

Captain, Alfred J. Wolff. *First Lieutenant,* Daniel E. Fitzpatrick. *Second Lieutenant,* Patrick Halpin.

First sergeant, William T. Keaveney; *quartermaster sergeant,* Thomas F. Bolger; *sergeants,* Edward A. Butler, Richard F. Dunne, Thomas F. Halliman, Bartholomew J. Collins.

Corporals, Thomas Magner, Peter W. Phelan, Edward L. Maloney, Edward Luddy, John Linehan, John Massey, William Clarken, Patrick H. Danaher.

Musicians: Joseph Hayden, (trumpeter) John F. Flaherty, Christopher Nolan.

Privates.

John R. Arrol,	John Holihan,	P. H. Phelan,
W. H. Beauchamp,	F. J. Hudner,	Jos. Phelan,
D. M. Casey,	J. F. Hanlon,	P. J. Phelan,
W. H. Carroll,	Thos. Kirk,	P. F. Quinn,
John J. Cullen,	F. W. Lawlor,	C. F. Roper,
D. F. Connor,	T. F. Lawlor,	C. C. Russell,
M. J. Crane,	W. H. Lynehan,	John Sullivan,
H. J. Crane,	Jas. McAvoy,	M. Sullivan,
Thos. R. Conlan,	F. W. Miller,	E. J. Shanahan,
John Dillan,	Edward Monaghan,	T. J. Shannahan,
Thos. Dillan,	M. J. McEvoy,	J. T. Sherman,
Jeremiah Dillan,	Timothy McEnerney,	D. P. Sullivan,
William Evans,	Jas. Magner,	J. J. Shea,
J. M. Fitzgerald,	C. B. Overton,	W. J. Vance,
W. J. Fitzgerald,	J. T. O'Donnell,	T. T. Whelahan.
J. W. Garde,		

www.ingramcontent.com/pod-product-compliance
Lightning Source LLC
Chambersburg PA
CBHW031122160426
43192CB00008B/1075